# PAUL
## and the
# THESSALONIANS

## Other Books by
## Abraham J. Malherbe

Gregory of Nyssa: The Life of Moses

The Cynic Epistles: A Study Edition

Social Aspects of Early Christianity

Moral Exhortation: A Greco-Roman Sourcebook

Abraham J. Malherbe

# PAUL
## and the
# THESSALONIANS

*The Philosophic Tradition of*
*Pastoral Care*

**FORTRESS PRESS**     **PHILADELPHIA**

*For*
*Ed and Peggy*

*Vir*
*Jannie en Rina*

Library of Congress Cataloging-in-Publication Data

Malherbe, Abraham J.
   Paul and the Thessalonians.

   Bibliography: p.
   Includes indexes.
   1. Bible. N.T. Thessalonians, 1st—Criticism, interpretation, etc. , 2. Paul, the Apostle, Saint—Contributions in pastoral theology.   3. Pastoral theology—Biblical teaching.   4. Church development, New—History.   5. Philosophy, Ancient.   I. Title.
BS2725.2.M35   1987      227'.8106      86–45918
ISBN 0–8006–1963–3

2661G86   Printed in the United States of America   1–1963

# Contents

# Preface

The relationship between early Christianity and the culture in which it took root has engaged my interest for some time. Initially I focused on the Christian effort, in its apologetic literature, to interpret itself to the larger society and defend itself against attacks. This book rather deals with the initial endeavor to form Christian communities in Greek and Roman society. Paul's first letter to the Thessalonians provides insight into how that took place as no other Christian document does. My long fascination with this letter has resulted in a number of articles of a technical nature and will come to fruition in a commentary on the Thessalonian correspondence in the Anchor Bible. Certain features of Paul's practice, however, cannot conveniently or systematically be examined in either articles or a commentary. The invitation to deliver the Haskell Lectures of 1985 at Oberlin College provided an opportunity to pull together some of the material that might illuminate Paul's method of founding and nurturing churches. This book is an expanded version of those lectures.

I wish to thank Professors Grover Zinn and Michael White for the invitation to deliver the lectures and for their and their colleagues' hospitality during a delightful week in Oberlin. I am grateful to John A. Hollar, my editor at Fortress Press, for his interest and for his contributions to the content and style of the book. Susan Garrett has been my right hand in preparing the lectures for publication. She has made valiant efforts to make the book intelligible, and only some of the time, I fear, succeeded in pressing me to clarify my thinking. For her collaboration I am thankful. I am indebted to my wife, Phyllis, for preparing the indexes.

Unless indicated otherwise in the footnotes, texts and translations of Greek and Latin authors are taken from the Loeb Classical Library (Cambridge: Harvard University Press; London: William Heinemann).

ABRAHAM J. MALHERBE
New Haven, Connecticut

# Abbreviations

| | |
|---|---|
| AGJU | Arbeiten zur Geschichte des antiken Judentums und des Urchristentums |
| *AJP* | *American Journal of Philology* |
| AnBib | Analecta Biblica |
| *ANRW* | *Aufstieg und Niedergang der römischen Welt*, ed. H. Temporini and W. Haase (Berlin and New York: Walter de Gruyter, 1972–) |
| APFenn | Acta philosophica fennica |
| *ARW* | *Archiv für Religionswissenschaft* |
| ASNU | Acta Seminarii neotestamentici upsaliensis |
| ATANT | Abhandlungen zur Theologie des Alten und Neuen Testaments |
| *BASOR* | *Bulletin of the American Schools of Oriental Research* |
| BET | Beiträge zur evangelischen Theologie |
| BETL | Bibliotheca Ephemeridum Theologicarum Lovaniensium |
| BFCT | Beiträge zur Forschung christlicher Theologie |
| *BZ* | *Biblische Zeitschrift* |
| *CPh* | *Classical Philology* |
| EB | Études bibliques |
| FRLANT | Forschungen zur Religion und Literatur des Alten und Neuen Testaments |
| *GRBS* | *Greek, Roman and Byzantine Studies* |
| GTA | Göttingen theologische Arbeiten |
| HNT | Handbuch zum Neuen Testament |
| HNTC | Harper's New Testament Commentary |
| *HR* | *History of Religions* |

| | |
|---|---|
| HTR | *Harvard Theological Review* |
| ICC | International Critical Commentary |
| JAC | *Jahrbuch für Antike und Christentum* |
| JBL | *Journal of Biblical Literature* |
| JETS | *Journal of the Evangelical Theological Society* |
| JHS | *Journal of Hellenic Studies* |
| JRH | *Journal of Religious History* |
| JTS | *Journal of Theological Studies* |
| KEK | Kritisch-Exegetischer Kommentar über das Neue Testament |
| MNTC | The Moffatt New Testament Commentary |
| MTZ | *Münchener theologische Zeitschrift* |
| MusHelv | *Museum Helveticum* |
| NCB | New Century Bible |
| NovT | *Novum Testamentum* |
| NovTSup | Novum Testamentum, Supplements |
| NTAbh | Neutestamentliche Abhandlungen |
| NTS | *New Testament Studies* |
| NTT | *Nederlands Theologisch Tijdschrift* |
| PG | Patrologia Graeca |
| PW | A. Pauly, G. Wissowa, and W. Kroll, eds., *Real-Encyclopädie der klassischen Altertumswissenschaft* |
| RAC | *Reallexikon für Antike und Christentum* |
| RB | *Revue biblique* |
| RhM | *Rheinisches Museum* |
| RHR | *Revue de l'histoire des religions* |
| RPh | *Revue de philologie* |
| RSR | *Religious Studies Review* |
| SBLDS | Society of Biblical Literature Dissertation Series |
| SBLMS | Society of Biblical Literature Monograph Series |
| SBLSBS | Society of Biblical Literature Sources for Biblical Study |
| SBLTT | Society of Biblical Literature Texts and Translations |
| SBS | Stuttgarter Bibelstudien |
| SCHNT | Studia ad Corpus Hellenisticum Novi Testamenti |
| SEA | *Svensk Exegetisk Arsbok* |
| SNT | Studien zum Neuen Testament |
| SNTSMS | Society for New Testament Studies Monograph Series |

| | |
|---|---|
| *ST* | *Studia Theologica* |
| *TAPA* | *Transactions of the American Philological Association* |
| *TDNT* | G. Kittel and G. Friedrich, eds., *Theological Dictionary of the New Testament* (Grand Rapids: Wm. B. Eerdmans, 1964–76) |
| *TZ* | *Theologische Zeitschrift* |
| WBC | World Bible Commentary |
| WMANT | Wissenschaftliche Monographien zum Alten und Neuen Testament |
| *ZNW* | *Zeitschrift für die neutestamentliche Wissenschaft* |
| *ZsysTh* | *Zeitschrift für systematische Theologie* |

# Introduction

This book deals with Paul's practice rather than his theology. It especially traces the way in which Paul established a church in the important city of Thessalonica, the capital city of the Roman province of Macedonia, maintained contact with it in order to ensure its continuing nurture, and instructed its members on how to care for one another. Rather than simply organize a church, Paul founded, shaped, and nurtured a community. In so doing, he was sensitive to the needs of individuals within the community who had committed themselves to new beliefs and a new way of life. Paul was, in fact, engaged in pastoral care, although he does not describe the enterprise in that manner.

Paul's method of organizing churches has frequently been examined, especially in studies devoted to his work as a missionary.[1] His self-understanding as a founder and minister to his churches has also received extensive treatment.[2] The focus of this book, however, is narrower than such studies. It has in view the pastoral work of Paul and his

1. See H. Wienel, *St. Paul: The Man and His Work*, trans. G. A. Bienemann (New York: G. P. Putnam's Sons, 1906), esp. 173–217; J. Warneck, *Paulus im Lichte der heutigen Heidenmission* (Berlin: Martin Warneck, 1913); M. Schlunk, *Paulus als Missionar* (Gütersloh: Bertelsmann, 1937); R. Allen, *Missionary Methods: Saint Paul's or Ours?* (reprint, Grand Rapids: Wm. B. Eerdmans, 1962); F. W. Maier, *Paulus als Kirchengründer und kirchlicher Organisator* (Würzburg: Echter-Verlag, 1961).

2. See esp. F. Laub, *Eschatologische Verkündigung und Lebensgestaltung nach Paulus. Eine Untersuchung zum Wirken des Paulus beim Aufbau der Gemeinde in Thessalonike* (Regensburg: Friedrich Pustet, 1973); idem, "Paulus als Gemeindegründer (I Thess)," in *Kirche im Werden. Studien zum Thema Amt und Gemeinde im Neuen Testament*, ed. J. Hainz (Munich: Ferdinand Schöningh, 1976), 17–38. See V. P. Furnish, "Theology and Ministry in the Pauline Letters," in *A Biblical Basis for Ministry*, ed. E. E. Shelp and R. Sunderland (Philadelphia: Westminster Press, 1981), 101–44. Furnish correctly emphasizes that Paul's theology and practice cannot be separated.

1

converts rather than his larger missionary strategy or his reflection on his apostleship. Furthermore, while acknowledging that Paul's ministry cannot be fully understood apart from his theology, we want to draw attention to pastoral practice in a particular Pauline church. Attempts have been made to examine the pastoral dimension of Paul's work, but they have been either too narrow in conception or sketchy in their treatment.[3] Recent sociological study of Paul has renewed interest in the formation and maintenance of the Pauline communities and has made significant contributions to our understanding of the matters pursued in this book.[4] This study has much in common with those attempts at social description, but it differs from them in being limited to one Christian community and in tracing the development of that community through the first months of its existence.

The church in Thessalonica lends itself to this kind of investigation. Not much more than eight months had passed between Paul's first arrival in Thessalonica and the writing of his first letter to his converts there. In the intervening period Paul had founded a church and made a number of efforts to shape it into a viable and vital community. First Thessalonians reflects this pastoral care of a fledgling church more clearly than any of Paul's other letters.[5]

Another major difference between this and other studies of Paul's pastoral concern is the manner in which Paul's methods will be

---

3. The only extensive treatment is W. E. Chadwick, *The Pastoral Teaching of St. Paul: His Ministerial Ideals* (Edinburgh: T. & T. Clark, 1907); it is outdated. See also C. F. G. Heinrici, *Paulus als Seelsorger,* Biblische Zeit- und Streitfrage 6/1 (Berlin: E. Runge, 1910); B. Bartmann, *Paulus als Seelsorger* (Paderborn: Ferdinand Schöningh, 1920); F. W. Beare, "St. Paul as Spiritual Director," in *Studia Evangelica II,* ed. F. L. Cross (Berlin: Akademie Verlag, 1964), 303–14; S. M. Gilmour, "Pastoral Care in the New Testament Church," *NTS* 10 (1964): 393–98; W. Barclay, "A Comparison of Paul's Missionary Preaching and Preaching to the Church," in *Apostolic History and the Gospel: Biblical and Historical Essays Presented to F. F. Bruce on His 60th Birthday,* ed. W. W. Gasque and R. P. Martin (Grand Rapids: Wm. B. Eerdmans, 1970), 165–75. From the orientation of pastoral theology, see R. Sullender, "Saint Paul's Approach to Grief: Clarifying the Ambiguity," *Journal of Religion and Health* 20 (1981): 63–74.

4. See esp. W. A. Meeks, *The First Urban Christians: The Social World of the Apostle Paul* (New Haven, Conn.: Yale Univ. Press, 1983); cf. B. Holmberg, *Paul and Power: The Structure of Authority in the Primitive Church as Reflected in the Pauline Epistles* (Philadelphia: Fortress Press, 1978).

5. Cf. G. Bornkamm, *Paul,* trans. D. M. G. Stalker (New York: Harper & Row, 1971), 63. See also R. F. Halamka, "I and II Thessalonians on Pastoral Care for Recent Converts" (Diss., Lutheran School of Theology, Chicago, 1975).

illuminated by the practices of his day.[6] The people to whom Paul writes had converted from paganism. In 1 Thessalonians it is striking how often Paul uses traditions and conventions that were appropriate to their background.[7] Paul's description of his ministry in 1 Thess. 2:1–8, for example, has distinct similarities to descriptions of ideal philosophers. A comparison between this passage and one from Dio Chrysostom, a younger contemporary of Paul, is instructive in this regard. Paul writes:

> For you yourselves know, brethren, that our visit to you was *not* in vain; *but* though we had already suffered and been shamefully treated at Philippi, as you know, we had courage (*eparrēsiasametha*) in our God to declare to you the gospel of God in the face of great opposition. For our appeal does *not* spring from error or uncleanness (*ex akatharsias*), *nor* is it made with guile (*oude en dolō*); *but* just as we have been approved by God to be entrusted with the gospel, so we speak, *not* to please men, but to please God who tests our hearts. For we *never* used either words of flattery (*kolakeias*), as you know, or a cloak for greed, as God is witness; *nor* did we seek glory (*doxan*) from men, whether from you or from others, though we might have made demands as apostles of Christ. *But* we were gentle among you, like a nurse taking care of her children. So, being affectionately desirous of you, we were ready to share with you *not only* the gospel of God *but also* our own selves, because you had become very dear to us.
>
> (1 Thess. 2:1–8)

After describing irresponsible Cynics and speakers who are intimidated by the mob, Dio distinguishes himself from them by describing the ideal philosopher:

> But to find a man who in plain terms (*katharōs*) and without guile (*adolōs*) speaks his mind with frankness (*parrēsiazomenon*), and *neither* for the sake of reputation (*doxēs*) nor for gain, *but* out of good will and concern for his fellow-men stands ready, if need be, to submit to ridicule and to the disorder and the uproar of the mob—to find such a man as that is *not* easy, *but* rather the good fortune of a very

6. For summaries of chaps. 1—3 of this book, see A. J. Malherbe, "Paul: Hellenistic Philosopher or Christian Pastor?" *American Theological Literary Proceedings* 39 (1985): 86–98; idem, "New Testament (Traditions and Theology of Care)," *Dictionary of Pastoral Care and Counseling*, ed. R. J. Hunter (Nashville: Abingdon Press, forthcoming).
7. For the traditions in general, see T. Holtz, "Traditionen im I. Thessalonicherbrief," in *Die Mitte des Neuen Testaments. Festschrift für Eduard Schweizer zum 70. Geburtstag*, ed. U. Luz and H. Weder (Göttingen: Vandenhoeck & Ruprecht, 1983), 55–78.

3

lucky city, so great is the dearth of noble, independent souls and such the abundance of toadies (*kolakōn*), mountebanks, and sophists. In my own case, for instance, I feel that I have chosen that role, *not* of my own volition, *but* by the will of some deity. For when divine providence is at work for men, the gods provide, *not* only good counsellors who need no urging, *but* also words that are appropriate and profitable to the listener.

(Dio Chrysostom *Discourse* 32.11–12)

The similarities between the descriptions by Paul and Dio include not only the content which they consider important in their self-descriptions but also the antithetic style ("not . . . but") in which they describe themselves. Dio was not unique among the philosophers in either his self-understanding, his concern to benefit others, or his description of himself, and Paul's readers must have been aware of the similarities between Paul's description of himself and the descriptions of the ideal philosopher.[8] Despite these similarities, however, there were also significant differences between the moral philosophers and Paul, and these differences must receive equal attention as we seek to gain a clearer understanding of Paul as pastor.[9]

A final comment on the manner in which the investigation will be conducted is in order. First Thessalonians is our major source of information for the process by which Paul first converted the Thessalonians, shaped them into a community, and then continued to exercise his care for them after he had been separated from them. The letter will be examined from these three perspectives, and a certain degree of repetition is unavoidable if we are to achieve a sense of the progression in Paul's work with his new converts.

8. For the similarities, see A. J. Malherbe, "'Gentle as a Nurse': The Cynic Background to I Thess ii," *NovT* 12 (1970): 203–17. Other descriptions of the ideal philosopher: Epictetus *Discourse* 3.22; Lucian *Demonax;* Maximus of Tyre *Discourse* 36. See K. Deissner, *Das Idealbild des stoischen Weisen,* Greifswalder Universitätsreden 24 (Greifswald: L. Bamberg, 1930); idem, "Das Sendungsbewusstsein der Urchristenheit," *ZsysTh* 7 (1930): 772–90. For the function of such depictions as self-descriptions, see K. Berger, "Hellenistische Gattungen im Neuen Testament," *ANRW* 2.25/2 (1984): 1135–36. Berger also adduces pseudo-Socrates *Epistle* 1. Relevant texts from the moralists are collected in A. J. Malherbe, *Moral Exhortation: A Greco-Roman Sourcebook,* Library of Early Christianity 4 (Philadelphia: Westminster Press, 1986). For an excellent description of the moralists, see S. Dill, *Roman Society from Nero to Marcus Aurelius* (New York: Macmillan, 1905), 289–383.

9. For some of the differences, see A. J. Malherbe, "Exhortation in First Thessalonians," *NovT* 25 (1983): 238–56.

# 1
# Founding the Christian Community

The picture of Paul's missionary strategy is fairly familiar and is usually derived in large measure from the biographical account in the Book of Acts. To begin with, Paul was an itinerant proclaimer of his message. At the end of the seven- or eight-year period (roughly A.D. 49–56) of the activity that is reflected in his letters, and about which we therefore know most,[1] he claims that he had fully preached the gospel "from Jerusalem and as far round as Illyricum" (Rom. 15:19). He had thus traveled from Jerusalem, along the coast of Syria, through Asia Minor, northern and southern Greece, all the way to the Adriatic.[2] Confining himself to the major routes that led from the east to Rome, he sought out the larger cities along them as points on which to concentrate. In Corinth he remained eighteen months (Acts 18:11), in Ephesus perhaps as long as three interrupted years; thus his activity in the other cities of the eastern Mediterranean basin was limited to at most a few months in each.

The cities in which Paul stayed over to establish churches were

1. This assumes the traditional chronology held, for example, by R. Jewett, *A Chronology of Paul's Life* (Philadelphia: Fortress Press, 1979). A chronology that dates the beginning of Paul's major work as early as the 30s and doubles the length of the period reflected in his letters is argued for by G. Luedemann, *Paul, Apostle to the Gentiles: Studies in Chronology*, trans. F. S. Jones (Philadelphia: Fortress Press, 1984).

2. We do not know when Paul preached in Illyricum. If he is referring to his own activity, it could have taken place during either his second or third missionary journey. A. Suhl (*Paulus und seine Briefe. Ein Beitrag zur paulinischen Chronologie*, SNT 11 [Gütersloh: Gerd Mohn, 1975], 92–94) suggests that Paul went as far west as Illyricum immediately after leaving Thessalonica. It is possible, however, that Paul considered the preaching of his converts to be an extension of his own and that in this sense his preaching had reached Illyricum.

5

politically, culturally, and economically important.[3] Christianity would radiate from these major cities to others and eventually penetrate into the countryside.[4] Just as significant as the prominence of these cities in the Roman provinces, of which they were often the capitals, was their location on the main thoroughfares of the Roman Empire. Their location guaranteed that their inhabitants would share in the mobility of Roman society.[5] Thus open to external influences, the cities were cosmopolitan in character. They teemed with devotees from assorted cults, including Jews, and wandering philosophers bent on reforming all whom they encountered. Thessalonica was such a city.[6] Situated on the Via Egnatia, with one of the best natural harbors in the Aegean, it was the most populous city of Macedonia and was known as the mother city of the entire province.[7] Inscriptions and other evidence reveal a city open to a stream of manual laborers, tradespeople, and persons of other occupations from Greece, Italy, and Asia Minor. When Paul arrived, the religious scene in the city was already richly diverse: the Egyptian divinities Isis, Serapis, and Osiris were well established in the city; the cult of Dionysus, and particularly that of the Cabiri, enjoyed great popularity; and there was a Jewish synagogue, about which Acts is our only source.[8] Inscriptional evidence locates a Samaritan synagogue there

3. A. von Harnack, *The Mission and Expansion of Christianity in the First Three Centuries,* trans. and ed. J. Moffatt, 2 vols. (New York: G. P. Putnam's Sons, 1909), 1:19–23; K. Holl, "Die Missionsmethode der alten und die der mittelalterlichen Kirche," *Gesammelte Aufsätze zur Kirchengeschichte,* 3 vols. (Tübingen: J. C. B. Mohr [Paul Siebeck], 1928), 3:118–19. This understanding of Paul's strategy was popularized by Allen, *Missionary Methods* (Introd., n. 1), 13–17.
4. On the urban character of Paul's churches, see Meeks, *First Urban Christians* (Introd., n. 4), esp. 9–50. For Christianity in the countryside, see Pliny *Epistle* 10.96; Justin Martyr *Apology I.* 67.3. Acts (13:49; 14:6) hints at the spread of Christianity beyond large cities during the first missionary journey, but that is part of Luke's emphasis on Christianity as a public, worldwide phenomenon. See A. J. Malherbe, "'Not in a Corner': Early Christian Apologetic in Acts 26:26," *The Second Century* 5 (1986).
5. On the physical mobility of Roman society, see Meeks, *First Urban Christians,* 16–19; A. J. Malherbe, *Social Aspects of Early Christianity,* 2d ed., enlarged (Philadelphia: Fortress Press, 1983), 62–65, 94–96.
6. W. Elliger, *Paulus in Griechenland. Philippi, Thessaloniki, Athen, Korinth,* SBS 92/93 (Stuttgart: Katholisches Bibelwerk, 1978), 78–114.
7. Antipater *Palatine Anthology* 10.428; cf. Strabo *Geography* 7.7.4; 7 frag. 21.
8. See C. Edson, "Cults of Thessalonica," *HTR* 41 (1948): 153–204; L. Robert, "Les inscriptions de Thessalonique," *RPh* 48 (1974): 180–246; R. Witt, "The Egyptian

in the fourth century; how much earlier Samaritans may have been in Thessalonica we do not know.[9] 

Paul himself fits the picture well; so also do some of his first converts and associates. Lydia, the seller of purple goods, whom he baptized in Philippi in northern Greece, was from Thyatira in Asia Minor (Acts 16:14–15). Aquila and Priscilla, whom he met and lived with in Corinth, were originally from Pontus on the Black Sea. They had earlier been expelled with the other Jews from Rome (Acts 18:2), would later go with Paul to Ephesus (Acts 18:18, 26; cf. 1 Cor. 16:19), and eventually would find their way back to Rome (Rom. 16:3). When Paul at the conclusion of his work in the eastern Mediterranean writes to the church in Rome, which he had not established or previously visited, he greets more than two dozen persons by name, many of whom he had known or worked with during this earlier phase of his career (Romans 16).[10] Of seventeen persons or groups of persons we know to have been associated with the church in Corinth, we meet nine while they are away from that city.[11] A considerable number of these persons may have been abroad, following where their trades or business led them, as were Aquila and Priscilla, Lydia, and a large segment of the society.

## THE SOCIAL SETTING OF PAUL'S PREACHING

The relative lack of residential permanence among those of Paul's converts important enough to receive mention sharpens the question as to how he went about establishing a firmly based church. Where did he begin missionizing in the cities? According to Acts, Paul headed for

---

Cults in Ancient Macedonia," in *Ancient Macedonia* (Thessalonica: Institute for Balkan Studies, 1977), 2:324–33; H. H. Hendrix, "Thessalonicans Honor Romans" (Diss., Harvard University, 1984); K. P. Donfried, "The Cults of Thessalonica and the Thessalonian Correspondence," *NTS* 31 (1985): 336–56.

9. B. Lifshitz and J. Schiby, "Une synagogue samaritaine à Thessalonique," *RB* 75 (1968): 368–78; E. Tov, "Une inscription grecque d'origine samaritaine trouvée à Thessalonique," *RB* 81 (1974): 394–99; J. D. Purvis, "The Paleography of the Samaritan Inscription from Thessalonica," *BASOR* 221 (1976): 121–23.

10. This assumes the integrity of the sixteen-chapter form of Romans, as argued for by H. Y. Gamble, *The Textual History of the Letter to the Romans: A Study in Textual and Literary Criticism* (Grand Rapids: Wm. B. Eerdmans, 1977).

11. See G. Theissen, *The Social Setting of Pauline Christianity: Essays on Corinth*, trans. and ed. J. H. Schütz (Philadelphia: Fortress Press, 1982), 91–96.

a Jewish synagogue whenever one was available.[12] There he would preach, dispute with the Jews, attract some converts (especially from among the nonproselyte Gentiles who had attached themselves in an uneasy relationship to the synagogue) and eventually be rejected. Harassed by Jews, he would be taken before civil authorities, and finally leave town for the next stop, his major work seemingly still undone. Doubts have been cast on the historical veracity of this standardized Acts account. It is so stock a presentation, and fits so neatly into Luke's own desire to provide a particular view of the relationship between Christianity and Judaism, that he has been suspected of forcefully imposing it on Paul.[13] Paul's own letters, furthermore, do not reflect a practice that was based in the synagogue.[14] Nevertheless, Paul's discipline by the synagogue (2 Cor. 11:24) and his seeking to convert Jews (1 Cor. 9:20) despite his belief that his field of labor was among the Gentiles (e.g., Rom. 15:15-21) together lend a degree of credence to the description in Acts.[15] But if we are to accept Paul's statements that he was sent to the Gentiles, we shall have to look for another location where he might have encountered the Gentiles whom he was commissioned to turn to God.[16]

Paul could have rented private quarters to preach in, as Acts has him do in Rome (Acts 28:16, 30), and he could have made use of accommodations like those of Tyrannus in Ephesus (Acts 19:9–10),

12. See Acts 13:14–51; 14:1–6; 17:1–9, 10–15, 17; 18:1–12, 19.
13. K. Löning, *Die Saulustradition in der Apostelgeschichte,* NTAbh N.F. 9 (Münster: Aschendorff, 1973); G. Bornkamm, "The Missionary Stance of Paul in I Corinthians 9 and Acts," in *Studies in Luke-Acts,* ed. L. E. Keck and J. L. Martyn (1966; reprint, Philadelphia: Fortress Press, 1980), 194–207; R. L. Brawley, "Paul in Acts: Lucan Apology and Conciliation," in *Luke-Acts: New Perspectives from the Society of Biblical Literature Seminar,* ed. C. H. Talbert (New York: Crossroad, 1984), 129–47. J. Jervell ("Paul in the Acts of the Apostles: Tradition, History, Theology," in *The Unknown Paul: Essays on Luke-Acts and Early Christian History* [Minneapolis: Augsburg Pub. House, 1984], 68–76) argues that Acts completes the picture of Paul presented in Paul's letters and that without Acts we cannot know the historical Paul.
14. Meeks, *First Urban Christians,* 26–27.
15. Central to the discussion is Gal. 2:9, on which see P. Stuhlmacher, *Das paulinische Evangelium. I. Vorgeschichte,* FRLANT 95 (Göttingen: Vandenhoeck & Ruprecht, 1968), 99 n. 5; Holmberg, *Paul and Power* (Introd., n. 4), 30; A. J. Hultgren, *Paul's Gospel and Mission: The Outlook from His letter to the Romans* (Philadelphia: Fortress Press, 1985), 128, 137–43.
16. See Meeks, *First Urban Christians,* 25–32.

which quite possibly could have been a guildhall or space he rented in which to lecture as a philosopher.[17] A widely held opinion is that Paul preached in the marketplaces and on street corners, in company with other wandering preachers, propagandists, and miracle workers, who were all competing for the same audience:[18]

> What would the ordinary citizen of a Hellenistic city have been likely to think if he came across Christian missionaries like Philip, Barnabas, or Paul preaching at a street corner or in a marketplace? The answer is: nothing out of the ordinary. He might even have gone out into the street to hear preaching of this kind. What Acts chapter 17 says of the Athenians was true of the people of the Mediterranean world in general: "All the Athenians and the foreigners who lived there spent their time in nothing except telling or hearing something new" (17:21). This taste was met by a host of wandering preachers who propagated their various schemes of salvation in the streets and markets of the cities and also in the staging posts of the great highways.[19]

The evidence to support this view, however, is problematic. It is ironic that appeal has to be made to Acts, which otherwise is given short shrift as a reliable source for Paul's practice. But even in Acts, despite his interest in depicting the public character of Christianity, Luke only very seldom locates Paul in public (cf. Acts 14:8–18). When in Acts Paul does show up in the marketplace in Athens, the Epicurean and Stoic philosophers take him from that hustle and bustle to the hill of Mars, a setting more conducive to calm discussion, where he is successful in making at least a few converts (Acts 17:16–34).[20] Thus the scene in Acts that best promises to support the hypothesis

17. See Malherbe, *Social Aspects*, 89–91.
18. This view has recently received wider currency as a result of D. Georgi, *Die Gegner des Paulus im 2. Korintherbrief. Studien zur religiösen Propaganda in der Spätantike*, WMANT 11 (Neukirchen: Neukirchener Verlag, 1964). See also H. Koester, *Introduction to the New Testament, vol. 1: History, Culture, and Religion of the Hellenistic Age* (Philadelphia: Fortress Press, 1982), 355–58. For a description of such preachers, see Dill, *Roman Society* (Introd., n. 8), 334–83.
19. D. Georgi, "Forms of Religious Propaganda," in *Jesus in His Time*, ed. H. J. Schultz (Philadelphia: Fortress Press, 1971), 124.
20. Luke's failure to describe Paul as conducting a campaign in the open air is the more striking in view of Luke's interest in the public character of Christianity. The statement in Acts 20:20 refers to Paul's teaching in the hall of Tyrannus (19:9–10), not to the marketplace. Acts 26:26 comes at the end of Paul's third defense and is apologetic. See Malherbe, "'Not in a Corner': Early Christian Apologetic in Acts 26:26," *The Second Century* 5 (1986).

of Paul as a marketplace preacher does not, on closer analysis, help to verify such a view.

A subsidiary bit of evidence for the hypothesis of Paul as marketplace preacher has been sought in the similarities between the style of such preachers and Paul's own style of oral discourse. The assumptions, never clearly demonstrated or connected, are as follows: The diatribe, a style of discourse developed by Cynics and then used by philosophers of all sorts, was used by the public preachers in their speeches to the crowds. In these speeches the preachers attempted to convert people to a new way of life. Paul clearly used elements of the diatribe in some of his letters, and since he too had made converts, the sections of his letters in which he uses the diatribal style must reflect the style he used when with live discourse he brought his hearers to conversion.[21] Therefore, since he shares both style and purpose with philosophers such as the Cynics, he must also have shared the social context in which they worked. Paul's apparent efforts to distinguish himself from such preachers (e.g., 1 Thess. 2:1–12) would indicate that his behavior made an identification between them possible.[22]

There are several difficulties with the hypothesis thus constructed. In a recent study Stanley Stowers has shown that, rather than the public square, the schoolroom was the place where the diatribe was developed and used, not only in speeches intended to bring about a radical change in the listeners' lives but also in teaching and philosophical exposition.[23] The letters in which Paul uses the diatribal style (e.g., Romans) are directed to churches he wanted to instruct or exhort, but not to convert, and if it were legitimate to infer a social context from the application of a particular style, the logical inference would be that Paul engaged his

---

21. See R. Bultmann, *Der Stil der paulinischen Predigt und die kynisch-stoische Diatribe*, FRLANT 13 (1910; reprint, Göttingen: Vandenhoeck & Ruprecht, 1984).

22. Thus M. Dibelius, *An die Thessalonicher I–II. An die Philipper*, HNT 11, 3d ed. (Tübingen: J. C. B. Mohr [Paul Siebeck], 1937), 7–11. For more detail and a different interpretation, see Malherbe, "'Gentle as a Nurse': The Cynic Background to I Thess ii," *NovT* 12 (1970): 203–17.

23. S. K. Stowers, *The Diatribe and Paul's Letter to the Romans*, SBLDS 57 (Chico, Calif.: Scholars Press, 1981).

readers as though they were students in a school rather than crowds in need of conversion.[24] Paul did describe himself in language used of moral philosophers, but that need not imply that he kept the company of the public preachers; there were also philosophers who kept to more private settings.[25] That his Christian opponents could attack him with barbs customarily hurled at Cynics of the lower sort means only that these competitors were accomplished in the art of invective.[26]

Stowers has also recently argued that

> public speaking and often the use of public buildings required status, reputation, and recognized roles which Paul did not have. Public speaking, on the one hand, often necessitated some type of legitimation or invitation or, on the other hand, demanded that the speaker somehow force himself on his audience,

as the Cynics did.[27] Stowers's protestation that it is difficult to imagine Paul entering into competition with the Cynics does not disprove the contention of other scholars that he did; more to the point is Stowers's argument that Paul, unlike the field preachers, did not primarily deliver an individualistic challenge to give up vice but aimed at forming a community of those who responded to his proclamation, for which a teacher-student relationship was necessary.[28] Such a relationship required a more secluded setting than the marketplace. Judging from pagan criticism of Christians in the second century, seclusion characterized Christians generally, not only those associated with Paul. Even these later critics rarely commented on the public behavior of Christians; rather, they condemned what they suspected went on in the private homes where Christians conducted

24. E. A. Judge ("The Early Christians as a Scholastic Community," *JRH* 1 [1960]: 4–15, 125–37) has sketched a picture of Pauline communities congenial to such an understanding.

25. See Malherbe, "'Gentle as a Nurse': The Cynic Background to I Thess ii," *NovT* 12 (1970): 203–17.

26. For Paul's use of such traditions in replying to attacks that were similarly couched in language derived from the philosophers and their opponents, see A. J. Malherbe, "Antisthenes and Odysseus, and Paul at War," *HTR* 76 (1983): 143–73.

27. S. K. Stowers, "Social Status, Public Speaking and Private Teaching: The Circumstances of Paul's Preaching Activity," *NovT* 26 (1984): 59–82.

28. Stowers, "Social Status," 80.

their worship services and made their converts.[29] As A. D. Nock observed, at an even later date Christians were still in the public mind but not in the public eye.[30]

The secluded setting in which Paul worked to found churches was provided by private homes. Acts gives a number of accounts of the conversion of entire households, or of Paul using a household as a base for his activities (e.g., 16:15, 31–34; 17:6–7; 18:1–8), and in his letters Paul frequently refers to churches in the home of one or another Christian (e.g., Rom. 16:3–4; 1 Cor. 1:14–16; 16:19; Philemon 2; cf. Col. 4:15). The subject has drawn considerable attention in recent years, and Michael White has now collected the relevant material of the first four centuries of the church's history and examined the significance of Christian houses as meeting places.[31]

## THE HOUSEHOLD OF JASON

Paul's correspondence with the Thessalonians does not provide detailed information on the social setting in which he first preached in their city. Acts 17:1–9 does, but its description is stereotypical: Paul preaches in the synagogue on three sabbaths and converts a few Jews, more devout Greeks, and a relatively large number of prominent women; his success prompts the Jews to foment a public uproar and lead an attack on the house of a certain Jason, where Paul and his associates are expected to be. When they are not found there, the Jews drag Jason and some of the Christians who are present before the local authorities and charge them with creating a civil disturbance and with sedition. The authorities place sufficient stock in these charges to require Jason and his friends to post bond before releasing them. Paul and his company are then

29. See Celsus, according to Origen *Against Celsus* 1.3; cf. 4.23; Minucius Felix *Octavius* 8.14. On Christian avoidance of publicity, see R. M. Grant, *Augustus to Constantine: The Thrust of the Christian Movement Into the Roman World* (New York: Harper & Row, 1970), 174–75, and Malherbe, "'Not in a Corner': Early Christian Apologetic in Acts 26:26," *The Second Century* 5 (1986), nn. 58–65.

30. A. D. Nock, *Conversion: The Old and the New in Religion from Alexander the Great to Augustine of Hippo* (Oxford: Clarendon Press, 1933), 192.

31. See Malherbe, *Social Aspects*, 60–112, 121–22; H.-J. Klauck, *Hausgemeinde und Hauskirche im frühen Christentum*, SBS 103 (Stuttgart: Katholisches Bibelwerk, 1981); idem, "Die Hausgemeinde und Hauskirche im Urchristentum," *MTZ* 32 (1981): 1–15; L. M. White, "Domus Ecclesiae: Domus Dei" (Diss., Yale University, 1982).

immediately sent by night to Beroea, where similar events occur (Acts 17:10–14).

When compared with 1 Thessalonians, this account presents several difficulties, only some of which need concern us. The major problem is that Acts mentions preaching in the synagogue only, while Paul writes to the Thessalonians as persons who had "turned from idols to serve the living and true God" (1 Thess. 1:9; cf. 2:14), that is, as persons who could not have been the converts mentioned in Acts 17:4. A period of evangelizing outside the synagogue should therefore be assumed, but Luke does not mention it. The reference to "three sabbaths," moreover, has been understood to apply to Paul's entire activity in Thessalonica, not just to his preaching in the synagogue, which would rule out a Gentile mission, for according to Acts, Paul turned to the Gentiles only after he had been rejected by the Jews (cf. Acts 13:46–47; 18:5–6).[32]

These difficulties, however, are not insuperable. The difficulties with the Acts account are caused by its stock character, which raises the suspicion that Luke created it out of whole cloth, and by its compressed nature. Luke provides a picture that serves his purpose but unfortunately not one that satisfies our curiosity. Nevertheless the account is more valuable than has sometimes been thought. To begin with, Acts 17:2 relates the three weeks to Paul's preaching in the synagogue, not to his entire sojourn in Thessalonica, which, judging from information in his letters, must have lasted as long as two or three months.[33] The grammar of the Acts account neither requires nor suggests a stay of merely three weeks, and, ironically (and this has not sufficiently been appreciated) Luke's stereotypical description of Paul's mission suggests that we should understand Jason's house as

32. The issues are discussed in detail in my forthcoming commentary on the letter in the Anchor Bible. For the argument that the converts mentioned in 1 Thess. 1:9 were God-fearers whom Paul had encountered in the synagogue, see Hultgren, *Paul's Gospel and Mission* (n. 15 above), 140–42.

33. While in Thessalonica, Paul supported himself by working with his hands in order not to burden his converts and in order to provide them with an example to imitate (1 Thess. 2:9; 4:9–12; cf. 2 Thess. 3:7–9). Paul's statements would be meaningful only if he had worked for at least a few weeks. In addition, he had received financial aid from Philippi on more than one occasion while he was in Thessalonica (Phil. 4:14). See E. Haenchen, *The Acts of the Apostles: A Commentary*, trans. B. Noble and G. Shinn (Philadelphia: Westminster Press, 1971), 511; and Suhl, *Paulus und seine Briefe* (n. 2 above), 103–7.

having been the base for Paul's work among the Gentiles after his separation from the synagogue, as Titius Justus's house would be in Corinth (cf. Acts 18:6–7).[34] It is obvious that Luke identifies a Christian group with Jason's establishment by the time Paul leaves the city. It remains for us to explore what is said of Jason and to discover how that group had come into existence.

This particular Jason is not mentioned elsewhere in the New Testament, so we are confined to what Acts tells us about him.[35] His Greek name need not exclude the possibility that he was a Jew, for Jews sometimes adopted the name as an alternative for Joshua. Acts, however, abruptly introduces him after what appears to have been Paul's break with the synagogue and presents him as under attack by the Jews, which may mean that Luke wants the reader to think of him as a Gentile. By the time Jason appears on the scene, there is a Christian congregation associated with his house, which presupposes some missionary activity on the part of Paul, for it is Paul who is the object of the mob's search. Unfortunately we do not know for certain who any of the "brethren" in the church were. Later in Acts we do hear of Aristarchus of Thessalonica (Acts 19:29; 20:4; 27:2), who, if he was the same person mentioned in Col. 4:10 (cf. Philemon 24), was a Jew. Demas, who is mentioned in Col. 4:14 and is associated with Thessalonica in 2 Tim. 4:10, was a Gentile. A Secundus of Thessalonica is simply mentioned (Acts 20:4). These individuals all appear on the scene during the third missionary journey, and there is no evidence that they were among the original members of the church. The information provided by Acts and the deutero-Pauline letters is therefore ambiguous as to

34. The compressed account in Acts 17:1–9 should be examined in the light of other accounts in Acts where Paul's founding of churches is described. Generally, a sequence of events is visualized in which Paul is rejected by the synagogue, turns to Gentiles, and (because of his success with them) brings about Jewish opposition (13:46–50; 18:5–17; cf. 16:12–40; 19:8–41), which modify the pattern. Most important to Luke are the beginning and the end of the sequence, and he passes over the intervening events in Thessalonica (cf. Haenchen, *Acts of the Apostles* [n. 33 above], 510). But the sudden appearance of Jason suggests that Luke wants the reader to understand that a similar sequence of events has occurred.

35. See G. Schille, *Die urchristliche Kollegialmission,* ATANT 48 (Zurich/Stuttgart: Zwingli Verlag, 1967), 49; W.-H. Ollrog, *Paulus und seine Mitarbeiter. Untersuchungen zu Theorie und Praxis der paulinischen Mission,* WMANT 50 (Neukirchen-Vluyn: Neukirchener Verlag, 1979), 30.

the ethnic constitution of the church in Thessalonica. We are driven back to Paul's own statements in 1 Thessalonians, which reflect a (largely?) Gentile congregation at the time of writing, a few months after the church's establishment.

Of special importance are the services Jason rendered Paul and the church. In the first place, he had extended hospitality to Paul and his companions, who included at least Silas and Timothy (Acts 17:7). Furthermore, other Christians openly congregated in Jason's house (Acts 17:6, 9). Together, they and Jason assumed legal responsibility for the Pauline delegation's activity by posting bond. All this assumes that Jason was a person of some means[36] and perhaps of some permanence in the city. His role was perhaps not unlike that of such patrons as Phoebe of Cenchraea (Rom. 16:2) and Gaius of Corinth (Rom. 16:23).[37] This fully accords with recent accounts of Paul's missionary strategy and analyses of the social makeup of his churches, which have drawn attention to the importance of such persons of means in the Pauline churches.[38]

Recent sociological investigation of the Pauline churches has focused to a large degree on Corinth, for we know more about the church there than about any other.[39] It is not unreasonable to work by way of analogy from Corinth to Paul's other churches, provided discipline is exercised and the tendency to generalize is properly curbed. In Corinth, Paul lived with Aquila and Priscilla, like himself tentmakers, and with them he plied his trade while evangelizing (Acts 18:1–4). It is likely that their business establishment was close to the commercial center of the city and that Paul's converts came from the artisans, tradespeople, and manual laborers with whom he would naturally come into contact. There is no direct evidence that Jason also was a

---

36. Cf. Meeks, *First Urban Christians*, 62–63.

37. On Phoebe, see Malherbe, *Social Aspects*, 98; E. A. Judge, "Cultural Conformity and Innovation in Paul: Some Clues from Contemporary Documents," The Tyndale Biblical Archaeology Lecture, 1983, 21. For the argument that Phoebe was more than a host, see E. Schüssler Fiorenza, *In Memory of Her: A Feminist Theological Reconstruction of Christian Origins* (New York: Crossroad, 1983), 170, 181–82. On Gaius, see Malherbe, *Social Aspects*, 73–74.

38. E.g., Theissen, *Social Setting* (n. 11 above), 83–91.

39. See Theissen, *Social Setting* (n. 11 above), 69–119; Malherbe, *Social Aspects* (n. 5 above), 71–77; Meeks, *First Urban Christians* (Introd., n. 4), 52–53, 67–72, 118–19.

tentmaker, nor that he had provided Paul with work, although neither suggestion is impossible or improbable.[40] What is important is Paul's reference to his work while in Thessalonica: "For you remember our labor and toil, brethren; we worked night and day, that we might not burden any of you, while we preached to you the gospel of God" (1 Thess. 2:9). When he then goes on to remind his readers of his pastoral care for the Christian community, it is natural to visualize a group in such a context as would be afforded by a Christian household. The view of 2 Thess. 3:7–9 that Paul worked with his hands to provide an example to the converts further implies such a setting, as does his discussion of their manual labor when he writes to them of brotherly love (1 Thess. 4:9–12). If the opportunity for this association was not provided by Jason, it must have been provided by someone like him. That in Acts the Christians are found in Jason's house, and that they jointly post bond, would seem to point to Jason as their host.

It is important that our view of the social constitution of the Thessalonian church *not* be influenced by the picture presented by Acts; it reflects Luke's tendency to mention socially prominent and economically well-off converts.[41] Jason's hospitality, the conversion of prominent women (Acts 17:4, cf. 12),[42] and the church's ability to post bail for Paul (17:9) reflect this same tendency, as does Luke's description of the Jewish opposition: jealous because of Paul's success in converting persons of prominent social standing, the Jews enlist good-for-nothings from the marketplace (*agoraioi*) and whip the crowd into an uproar. The term *agoraios* frequently is used in ancient literature to describe persons of low birth, who are then contrasted with the nobility or upper classes, as

40. K. Lake and H. J. Cadbury, *The Beginnings of Christianity*, 5 vols. (London: Macmillan, 1933), 4:205; Haenchen, *Acts of the Apostles* [n. 33 above], 512; R. F. Hock, *The Social Context of Paul's Ministry: Tentmaking and Apostleship* (Philadelphia: Fortress Press, 1980), 31.

41. Malherbe, *Social Aspects*, 30f.; idem, "'Not in a Corner': Early Christian Apologetic in Acts 26:26," *The Second Century* 5 (1986). See, e.g., Acts 6:7; 8:26; 10:1; 18:8.

42. See also Acts 9:36–43; 12:12; 16:14–15; 18:26. Cf. M. Hengel, "Maria Magdalena und die Frauen als Zeugen," in *Abraham unser Vater*, ed. O. Betz, M. Hengel, and P. Schmidt, AGJU 5 (Leiden: E. J. Brill, 1963), 243–56; Schüssler Fiorenza, *In Memory of Her* (n. 37 above), 167. Jervell ("The Daughters of Abraham: Women in Acts," in *The Unknown Paul* [n. 13 above]) wrongly argues that they are subordinate.

here.[43] Significant for our purpose is that *agoraios* in such contexts retains its association with the marketplace (*agora*) and the small tradespeople and manual laborers who gathered there, whom it describes pejoratively.[44] Against this background, Luke's usage is remarkable. Not only does he attribute the Jewish opposition to the social factor of competition for converts of high status but in this social conflict he portrays the Jews' allies as recruited from the class of persons represented by manual laborers. Luke knows of Paul's manual labor (Acts 18:3; 20:18-35) but for some reason chooses not to mention it in Thessalonica, precisely where it was of major importance to Paul. Rather, he prefers to depict a Macedonian church that was anything but poor or made up of manual laborers (contrast 2 Cor. 8:2).

## PAUL IN THE WORKSHOP

If indeed the household provided the primary context for Paul's evangelization in Thessalonica, as argued above, then it is necessary to ask in what way such a household would have been appropriate both as a workshop and an appropriate setting for preaching and teaching. The residence in view was most probably not a *domus*, which could be afforded only by the extremely wealthy, but housing in an *insula*, a type of apartment house that served the vast majority of people in the large cities of the Roman Empire.[45] A typical *insula* would contain a row of shops on the ground floor, facing the street, and provide living accommodations for the owners and their families over the shop or in the rear. Also on the premises would be space for the manufacturing of goods sold in the shops, and living quarters for visitors, employees, and servants or slaves. These households were therefore quite unlike the modern nuclear family. They represented a considerable cross section of a major portion of society, made up of manual laborers and

43. E.g., Plutarch *Aemilius Paulus* 38.3; Dio Chrysostom *Discourse* 1.33; cf. Horace *The Art of Poetry* 244-50 for the Latin equivalent (*forensis*).

44. E.g., Plato *Protagoras* 347C; Dio Chrysostom *Discourses* 22.1; 27.5; 32.9; 36.25; 66.25; Lucian *Philosophies for Sale* 27.

45. See. A. G. McKay, *Houses, Villas and Palaces in the Roman World* (London: Thames & Hudson, 1975), esp. 213-14; D. C. Verner, *The Household of God and the Social World of the Pastoral Epistles,* SBLDS 71 (Chico, Calif: Scholars Press, 1983), chap. 2, esp. 57, 59.

tradespeople. Such households were part of an intricate social network, being linked to other households by ties of kinship, friendship, professional advantage, and so on. Paul's strategy of initiating his work in such households was a sound one, because the household provided him with a relatively secluded setting and a ready-made audience as well as a network along which his influence could spread.[46]

A century and a quarter after Paul, Celsus, an enemy of Christianity, presents a view of Christians that conforms to this reconstruction:

> In private houses also we see wool-workers, laundry-workers, and the most illiterate and bucolic yokels, who would not dare to say anything at all in front of their elders and more intelligent masters . . . . (Children, they say,) should leave father and their schoolmasters, and go along with the women and little children who are their play-fellows to the wooldresser's shop, or to the cobblers or the washerwoman's shop, that they may learn perfection. And by saying this they persuade them.[47]
>
> (Origen *Against Celsus* 3.55)

Celsus therefore knows of Christian evangelism occurring in private houses, where the working class practice their trades or conduct their business. To this Origen responds, not by denying the accuracy of Celsus's depiction of Christian activity, but by stressing the salutary effects of the Christian teaching.

The Christian practice was similar to that of some philosophers who preached to the masses. Celsus's invective to a degree resembles that of his contemporary, Lucian of Samosata. Lucian lambastes the Cynics, whom he associates with manual laborers. Speaking as "Philosophy," he says of them:

> There is an abominable class of men, for the most part slaves and hirelings, who had nothing to do with me in childhood for lack of leisure, since they were performing the work of slaves or hirelings or learning such trades as you would expect their like to learn—cobbling, building, busying themselves with fullers' tubs, or carding wool to

46. For Paul in the workshop, see Hock, *Social Context* (n. 40 above), chap. 3. For the network provided by the household, see Meeks, *First Urban Christians*, 29–31, 75–77; L. M. White, "Adolf Harnack and the 'Expansion' of Christianity: A Reappraisal of Social History," *The Second Century* 5 (1985/86): 97–127.

47. Trans. H. Chadwick, *Origen: Contra Celsum* (Cambridge: Cambridge Univ. Press, 1953), 165–66.

make it easy for the women to work, easy to wind, and easy to draw off when they twist a yarn or spin a thread.

(Lucian *The Runaways* 12)

In another scene, Lucian has Zeus speak to Justice of the dress and numbers of the Cynics:

> But at present, do you not see how many short cloaks and staves and wallets there are? On all sides there are long beards, and books in the left hand, and everybody preaches in favor of you; the public walks are full of people assembling in companies and in battalions, and there is nobody who does not want to be thought a scion of Virtue. In fact, many, giving up the trades they had before, rush after the wallet and cloak, tan their bodies in the sun to Ethiopian hue, make themselves extemporaneous philosophers out of cobblers or carpenters, and go about praising you and your virtue. Consequently, in the words of the proverb, it would be easier for a man to fall in a boat without hitting a plank than for your eye to miss a philosopher wherever it looks.[48]

(Lucian *The Double Indictment* 6)

As Lucian's comments illustrate, itinerant philosophers frequently made their converts from persons of the artisan class, who then abandoned their trades or who were at least accused of doing so, in order themselves to become itinerant preachers. The setting in which Lucian places the itinerant philosophers is, however, public—unlike the workshop in a household where we have placed Paul in Thessalonica. But we do know of philosophers who taught in workshops. Socrates was remembered as teaching in the workshops and the marketplace,[49] men like the Cynic Micyllus plied their trade while engaged in teaching,[50] Crates is found reading in Philiscus's shop while the latter stitches away at his shoes,[51] and Simon the Shoemaker caught the imagination of a later age as a person who typified the philosopher-worker who attracted to himself for discussion philosophers of various persuasions.[52] So too, in the later literature not only

---

48. See also Lucian *The Runaways* 17, 28, 33; Lucian *Icaromenippus* 30–31.
49. Diogenes Laertius *Lives of Eminent Philosophers* 2.21, 122.
50. Lucian *The Downward Journey* 14–29.
51. Teles, *Fragment* 4B. See E. O'Neil, *Teles: The Cynic Teacher*, SBLTT 11 (Missoula, Mont.: Scholars Press, 1977), 48, 21–31.
52. Pseudo-Socrates *Epistles* 8; 9.4; 11; 13.1; 18.2. See R. F. Hock, "Simon the Shoemaker as an Ideal Cynic," *GRBS* 17 (1976): 41–53.

Socrates but also his followers Antisthenes and Aristippus were brought into contact with Simon.[53]

It should be acknowledged that these philosophers from an earlier age represented an ideal that not many people were inclined to realize in their own practice. Nevertheless we do have examples of philosophers contemporary with Paul who engaged in manual labor and used the opportunity to instruct their disciples. For example, Musonius Rufus, banished to Gyara, thought it valuable that the philosopher work with his hands so that his students might be benefited

> by seeing him at work in the fields, demonstrating by his own labor the lesson which philosophy inculcates—that one should endure hardships, and suffer the pains of labor with his own body, rather than depend upon another for sustenance.[54]
>
> (Musonius Rufus *Fragment* 11)

Musonius did not work in a shop, but Philiscus and Simon taught the same lessons of hardihood and self-sufficiency as they cobbled in their workshops.

It is against this background that we should view Paul's manual labor in Thessalonica.[55] Paul first refers to his work in a description of his missionary labor among the Thessalonians in which he draws on language commonly used to describe the better sort of philosopher. There is insufficient reason to suppose that the description is no more than literary convention which does not reflect his actual practice. The point is rather that Paul fixes his manual labor in a setting that had distinct analogies to a philosophical ideal of his day.[56] Of major significance to the instruction that went on in such settings was the elevation of the philosopher as a model for his disciples to follow. This was also true in Paul's case, and we shall return to this subject in chapter 2.

53. E.g., pseudo-Socrates, *Epistle* 13.1.
54. Trans. C. E. Lutz, *Musonius Rufus: "The Roman Socrates,"* Yale Classical Studies 10 (New Haven, Conn.: Yale Univ. Press, 1947), 83.
55. For the argument that this background rather than rabbinic practice illuminates Paul's practices, see Hock, *Social Context* (n. 40 above).
56. See, e.g., Dio Chrysostom *Discourse* 32.11 and the discussion in Malherbe, "'Gentle as a Nurse': The Cynic Background to I Thess ii," *NovT* 12 (1970): 203–17.

## THE PHILOSOPHERS' CALL
## TO CONVERSION

The philosophers' aim was to benefit their listeners by turning them to the rational life or to convert them to philosophy (i.e., to educate them morally). Serious philosophers shared the view that human beings fall short of their potential to live rationally and thus morally, but they differed in their assessment of the gravity of the human condition. Stoics, in general, had the optimistic view that people have a natural disposition to virtue. According to the Stoics, ignorance and misunderstanding are the causes of human error but can be overcome by proper instruction when it is applied with discrimination.[57] Some Cynics too shared this view,[58] but others of them were pessimistic, holding that the majority of people were so diseased in soul and morally corrupt that the only hope of cure lay in the severest treatment, with no concession made to the individual's circumstances.[59] What philosophers shared, however, was the assumption that people were generally able to change and that the philosopher could bring about change through his speech.[60]

57. E.g., Musonius Rufus *Fragments* 2; 3; 10; cf. A. C. Van Geytenbeek, *Musonius Rufus and Greek Diatribe* (Assen: Van Gorcum, 1963), 18, 28–33. On the proper attitude toward the erring, see Epictetus *Discourse* 1.18.3–11.

58. E.g., Lucian *Demonax* 10; cf. Malherbe, "'Gentle as a Nurse': The Cynic Background to I Thess ii," *NovT* 12 (1970): 210–11; and I. M. Nachov, "Der Mensch in der Philosophie der Kyniker," in *Der Mensch als Mass der Dinge,* ed. R. Mueller (Berlin: Akademie Verlag, 1976), 361–98.

59. E.g., pseudo-Diogenes *Epistles* 28; 29; pseudo-Heraclitus *Epistles* 2; 4; 5; 7; 9; pseudo-Hippocrates *Epistle* 7. On the misanthropy of these Cynics, see G. A. Gerhard, *Phoinix von Kolophon* (Leipzig/Berlin: Teubner, 1909), 67–68; A. J. Malherbe, "Medical Imagery in the Pastoral Epistles," in *Texts and Testaments: Critical Essays on the Bible and Early Church Fathers,* ed. W. Eugene March (San Antonio, Tex.: Trinity Univ. Press, 1980), 19–35; idem, "Self-Definition Among Epicureans and Cynics," in *Jewish and Christian Self-Definition,* ed. B. F. Meyer and E. P. Sanders (Philadelphia: Fortress Press, 1982), 3:52–54. For taking into consideration a person's disposition and circumstances, see Malherbe, "'In Season and Out of Season': 2 Timothy 4:2," *JBL* 103 (1984): 235–43.

60. Even philosophers with a generally optimistic view, however, discovered that some people are impossible to persuade. Cf. Epictetus *Discourse* 2.15.13–20, and see B. L. Hijmans, *ASKESIS: Notes on Epictetus' Educational System* (Assen: Van Gorcum, 1959), 4, 32; Seneca *Epistle* 94.24, on which see I. Hadot, *Seneca und die griechisch-römische Tradition der Seelenleitung* (Berlin: Walter de Gruyter, 1969), 151–52; Lucian *Demonax* 10.

Although philosophers also wrote, the spoken word received their highest praise.[61] They regarded hearing as the most rational of the senses.[62] And so the philosopher would drag the crowds to him by their ears as he delivered his protreptic speeches to convert them.[63] Stoic philosophers such as Dio Chrysostom claimed that the gods, as part of their providence, provided counselors who acted of their own will as well as words that were appropriate to their hearers. While the gods do speak through oracles, according to Dio, their communication through men, in strong, full utterance and in clear terms, instructing listeners in the most vital matters with purpose and persuasiveness, is far superior.[64] The philosopher's speech is further superior to that of the sophists:

> The words and all the sophistries of men are worth nothing compared to the inspiration and speech that come from the gods. Indeed, whatever wise and true words about the gods and the universe there are to be found among men, none have ever lodged in human souls except by the divine will and Fortune through the early prophets and divine men.
>
> (Dio Chrysostom *Discourse* 1.57)

Dio at times uses the convention of appealing to the gods for guidance at the beginning or end of a speech,[65] but his notion of inspiration is not to be understood as simply part of that convention. He represents the Stoic view that as the philosopher is a helper sent by God,[66] so are his words.[67] Although the philosopher is moved by goodwill and friendship toward his listeners, he speaks in the

---

61. E.g., Plato *Phaedrus* 275C–277A; Dio Chrysostom *Discourses* 1.8; 18.2–3; 19.3. See H. Karpp, "Viva Vox," in *Mullus. Festschrift Theodor Klauser*, ed. A. Stuiber and A. Hermann, JAC Ergänzungsband 1 (Münster: Aschendorff, 1964), 190–99.

62. Plutarch *On Listening to Lectures* 38A.

63. For dragging by the ears, see Lucian *Heracles* 3; 5; 8; cf. *The Scythian* 11; Diogenes Laertius *Lives of Eminent Philosophers* 7.24. Examples of protreptic speech: Horace *Satire* 2.3; Dio Chrysostom *Discourse* 1; Maximus of Tyre *Discourse* 36 (trans. Malherbe, in *Moral Exhortation* [Introd., n. 8], 73–79).

64. On the superiority to oracles, cf. Dio Chrysostom *Discourse* 34.4–5; Epictetus *Discourse* 3.1.36–37. See E. Wilmes, "Beiträge zur Alexandrinerrede (or. 32) des Dion Chrysostomos" (Diss., Bonn, 1970), 13–23.

65. See Dio Chrysostom *Discourses* 34.4–5; 38.9, 51; 39.8; 45.1; 49.3; cf. Demosthenes *Epistle* 1.1; Iamblichus *Life of Pythagoras* 1.

66. Cf. Epictetus *Discourses* 3.21.11–18; 22.2, 23, 53, and see p. 4.

67. Dio Chrysostom *Discourse* 32.14.

presence of Zeus,[68] and it is God who gives him the courage (*tharrēsai*) to speak when he is violently opposed.[69] The philosopher's speech should always be useful and profitable, aimed at purifying and curing listeners by bringing them to their senses. His words are arrows aimed at the soul.[70] The human condition is frequently described in medical terms, and the philosopher is represented as a physician who through his speech operates and cauterizes, or administers drugs and honey, always adapting the cure to the condition of the patient.[71] Cynic philosophers with a pessimistic view of the human condition, however, were known for the unrelieved harshness of their speech and for abusiveness which stung like wasps and bit like dogs.[72] Although the moral philosophers distinguished themselves from the sophists, some nevertheless reflected on the proper style of speech, and all extolled frankness (*parrēsia*), which held back nothing in the pursuit to benefit the listeners.[73]

---

68. Dio Chrysostom *Discourse* 12.12.
69. Dio Chrysostom *Discourse* 32.21.
70. Speech as profitable: Dio Chrysostom *Discourses* 32.12; 34.5; 38.2; Plutarch *On Listening to Lectures* 42A; Julian *Oration* 6.201C. As purifying: Dio Chrysostom *Discourse* 57.9; Plutarch *On Listening to Lectures* 42BC, *How to Tell a Flatterer from a Friend* 59D, and *Progress in Virtue* 82C; Lucian *Philosophies for Sale* 8. As curing: Dio Chrysostom *Discourse* 32.18–19; Plutarch *How to Tell a Flatterer from a Friend* 59DE; pseudo-Diogenes *Epistle* 29.1, 4. As restoring to senses: Dio Chrysostom *Discourses* 51.4; 77/78.39; Plutarch *On Listening to Lectures* 42A. Arrows: Lucian *Heracles* 6; 8; *Nigrinus* 35–37.
71. See Malherbe, "Medical Imagery" (n. 59 above). Philosopher as physician operating and cauterizing: Cicero *On Duties* 1.136; Seneca *Epistles* 52.9; 75.6–8; Dio Chrysostom *Discourse* 77/78.43–45; Plutarch *On Listening to Lectures* 46E–47B; pseudo-Diogenes *Epistles* 28.7; 29.5. On the philosopher's lecture room as a hospital for sick souls: Epictetus *Discourse* 3.23.30. Administering drugs: Dio Chrysostom *Discourse* 57.5; Plutarch *How to Tell a Flatterer from a Friend* 55C; Julian *Oration* 8.243D. Honey (thought to have therapeutic qualities): Dio Chrysostom *Discourses* 9.6; 33.16; cf. 57.8–9; Plutarch *How to Tell a Flatterer from a Friend* 59D; *Fragment* 203; Stobaeus *Anthology* 3.13.68. Adapting the cure: Seneca *Epistle* 64.6–10; Themistius *Oration* 22 (67, 4–6 Downey-Norman).
72. Harshness: Plutarch *How to Tell a Flatterer from a Friend* 69C. Abusiveness: Epictetus *Discourse* 3.22.10, 50; Dio Chrysostom *Discourse* 32.11; Lucian *Peregrinus* 18; Stobaeus *Anthology* 3.13.59. Stinging: Dio Chrysostom *Discourse* 8.3. Biting: Demetrius *On Style* 259–61; Plutarch *How to Tell a Flatterer from a Friend* 67A.
73. Proper style: Seneca *Epistles* 40; 59.4–7; 75.1–7; 100; 114; 115.1–2, 18. See G. H. Müller, *Animadversiones ad L. Annaei Senecae epistulas quae sunt de oratione spectantes* (Inaug. Diss., Thuringia, 1910); M. Pohlenz, *Die Stoa. Geschichte einer geistigen Bewegung*, 2 vols., 4th ed. (Göttingen: Vandenhoeck & Ruprecht, 1970), 2:31; Hadot, *Seneca* (n. 60 above), 109–10. Cf. also Epictetus *Discourse* 3.23.33–37. Frankness: see E. Peterson, "Zur Bedeutungsgeschichte von *Parresia*," in *Reinhold*

Philosophic speeches took aim at human error or sins, which were thought to result from ignorance.[74] The speeches frequently began by listing vices, which revealed the true condition of the listeners, before setting about to correct them.[75] The philosopher's speech sought to agitate the listener and create dissatisfaction with his sinful condition. According to Epictetus, every error involves a contradiction or conflict. As long as a person is involved in contradiction, that is, erring while wishing to do right, but does not understand that he is involved in contradiction, he will continue in that state. The philosopher's task is to lay bare through speech the condition that is the cause of error.[76] By bringing to light the inconsistency that exists, the philosopher hopes to disturb his listeners and bring them to a realization of their condition.[77] Confession or acknowledgment of one's error is necessary for progress,[78] because knowledge of error is the beginning of salvation.[79]

The person who listened to a philosopher's speech was expected, but not absolutely required, to have the right disposition if he was to receive any benefit.[80] When he was receptive, the effect could be

*Seeberg—Festschrift*, vol. 1: *Zur Theorie des Christentums*, ed. W. Koepp (Leipzig: Scholl, 1929), 283–97; H. Schlier, "Parrēsia, parrēsiazomai," *TDNT* 5 (1967): 871–86; Malherbe, "'Gentle as a Nurse': The Cynic Background to I Thess ii," *NovT* 12 (1970): 208–16. Holding nothing back: pseudo-Plato *Clitophon* 407A; Dio Chrysostom *Discourses* 13.16; 77/78.33, 42, 45; Plutarch *How to Tell a Flatterer from a Friend* 60C. Cf. Acts 20:20, 27. The Cynics intoned their practice of speaking openly in public (*en mesō*): Epictetus *Discourse* 3.22.25; Dio Chrysostom *Discourse* 35.4; Lucian *Peregrinus* 8; Diogenes Laertius *Lives of Eminent Philosophers* 6.69; Julian *Oration* 7.210B.

74. E.g., Dio Chrysostom *Discourse* 32.33; Epictetus *Discourse* 1.26.7

75. The philosopher's speech as showing or disclosing error: Dio Chrysostom *Discourses* 33.13; 72.13; Plutarch *Progress in Virtue* 82A. Correction of vices: Dio Chrysostom *Discourse* 13.14–28, and at the beginnings of *Discourses* 14; 16; 17; 24; 27; 66; 68; 69; 71; cf. pseudo-Crates *Epistle* 15. Vice lists were also used more particularly to depict a person's condition before conversion (e.g., Lucian *The Double Indictment* 17) and in setting forth the choice between virtue and vice (e.g., Maximus of Tyre *Discourse* 36.4C).

76. Epictetus *Discourse* 2.26. See Stowers, *The Diatribe* (n. 23 above), 56–57.

77. Epictetus *Discourse* 3.23.33–37.

78. Cf. Seneca *Epistle* 53.8; Plutarch *Progress in Virtue* 82AE.

79. Cf. Seneca *Epistle* 28.9; see Hadot, *Seneca* (n. 60 above), 162–64. According to Plutarch *On Listening to Lectures* 46E, it is one's natural sense of shame that is the beginning of salvation; see W. Schmid, "Contritio und 'ultima linea rerum' in neuen epikureischen Texten," *RhM* 100 (1957): 310.

80. Cf. Dio Chrysostom *Discourses* 1.8, 10; 72.11; Plutarch *On Listening to Lectures*. Polemo (see p. 27) is an example of someone converting to philosophy without having come to the philosopher with a proper attitude.

dramatic. Dio Chrysostom's account of Diogenes's speech to Alexander, in which Diogenes pressed Alexander to come to self-knowledge, illustrates the philosopher's technique as well as the desired effect of the speech:

> So when Diogenes perceived that he was greatly excited and quite keyed up in mind with expectancy, he toyed with him and pulled him about in the hope that somehow he might be moved from his pride and thirst for glory and be able to sober up a little. For he noticed that at one time he was delighted, and at another grieved, at the same thing, and that his soul was as unsettled as the weather at the solstices when both rain and sunshine come from the very same source.
>
> (Dio Chrysostom *Discourse* 4.77–78)

The person who listened to a philosopher's speech was expected to respond emotionally as well as rationally. He could shudder, feel ashamed, repent, and experience joy and wonder, "and even have varying facial expressions and changes of feeling as the philosopher's speech affects him and touches his recognition of that part of his soul which is sound and that which is sick."[81]

Normally, conversion was probably a gradual process.[82] It could be brought about by such life-wrenching experiences as shipwreck[83] or exile, during which a person might discover new values and commit himself to a different way of life.[84] The accounts of conversion in response to speeches, however, tend to stress that conversion was

---

81. Musonius Rufus *Fragment* 49. Cf. Plutarch *How to Study Poetry* 36E and *On Listening to Lectures* 46D.

82. Cf. A. D. Nock, "Bekehrung," *RAC* 2 (1954): 107–8. For more extended treatments of conversion, see Nock, *Conversion* (n. 30 above); idem, "Conversion and Adolescence," in *Essays on Religion and the Ancient World*, ed. Z. Stewart (Cambridge, Mass.: Harvard Univ. Press, 1972), 1:469–80.

83. For the example of Zeno, see Plutarch *How to Profit by One's Enemies* 87A and *On Tranquility of Mind* 467CD, and Seneca *On Tranquility* 14.3; Diogenes Laertius *Lives of Eminent Philosophers* 7.4. See L. Sternbach, *Gnomologium Vaticanum*, Texte und Kommentare 2 (reprint, Berlin: Walter de Gruyter, 1963), 114–15, for attribution of the story to other philosophers.

84. For Diogenes, see Plutarch *How to Profit by One's Enemies* 87A; Diogenes Laertius *Lives of Eminent Philosophers* 6.49; Musonius Rufus *Fragment* 9. For Crates, see Plutarch *How to Profit by One's Enemies* 87A. Dio Chrysostom *Discourse* 13 provides an account of his own conversion during his banishment. For a revisionistic treatment of it, see J. L. Moles, "The Career and Conversion of Dio Chrysostom," *JHS* 98 (1978): 79–100.

instantaneous.[85] This may be due to the protreptic function of such accounts.[86] They were recounted as examples of people who were decisive,[87] prepared to make a complete break with their past,[88] and therefore worthy of emulation. The terminology used to describe conversion—to turn, begin a new life, awake and become sober, experience a metamorphosis, and repent[89]—conveys the radical reorientation expected in conversion, which may result in giving up one's marriage, children, and country, or changing one's profession.[90]

The above features of conversion, but in particular the redefinition of personal identity, the suddenness with which it occurs, and the

85. E.g., Plutarch *The Stoics and the Poets* 1057EF and *Reply to Colotes* 1117B. For the controversy on the topic, see Nock, "Bekehrung," *RAC* 2 (1954): 107–8; Malherbe, "'Not in a Corner': Early Christian Apologetic in Acts 26:26," *The Second Century* 5 (1986), nn. 76–83.

86. Cf. Olof Gigon, "Antike Erzählungen über die Berufung zur Philosophie," *MusHelv* 3 (1946): 10–11.

87. E.g., Maximus of Tyre *Discourse* 36.4. The prime example is Heracles at the crossroads: Xenophon *Memorabilia* 2.1.21–34; cf. Dio Chrysostom *Discourse* 1.58–84; pseudo-Diogenes *Epistle* 30; and see A. J. Malherbe, "Herakles," *RAC* (forthcoming). Cf. also Epictetus *Discourses* 3.21.11–12; 22.12, 53, 66; Julian *Oration* 6.182A.

88. On the present moment (*nun*) as the time to change and abandon the earlier (*tote*) life, see Epictetus *Discourses* 3.22.10, 13, 20; 4.4.6; cf. 3.21.23; Diogenes Laertius *Lives of Eminent Philosophers* 6.56. Cf. also A.-J. Festugière, *Epicurus and His Gods*, trans. C. W. Chilton (Cambridge, Mass.: Harvard Univ. Press, 1956), 39.

89. Turning: (*Epistrephein*): Epictetus *Discourses* 3.16.15; 22.39; 23.16, 37; 4.4.7; Lucian *The Double Indictment* 17. Generally, the *epistrophē* is a turning to oneself, coming to one's senses, but it also describes a turning to philosophy (e.g., pseudo-Diogenes *Epistle* 34.1) and honoring the divine (e.g., Epictetus *Discourse* 2.20.22). Beginning a new life: Marcus Aurelius, *Meditations* 7.2. Awaking or becoming sober: Seneca *Epistle* 53.8; Lucian *The Double Indictment* 17. Metamorphosis: Seneca *Epistle* 6.1 (cf. G. Maurach, *Der Bau von Senecas Epistulae Morales* [Heidelberg: Carl Winter, 1970], 41 n. 58 and the literature cited there); 94.48. Repenting: (*metanoein*): Plutarch *How to Tell a Flatterer from a Friend* 56A, 74C. According to Nock (*Conversion* [n. 30 above], 180), *metanoia* is an intellectual value judgment. Important for our topic is pseudo-Cebes *Tabula* 10–11; see J. T. Fitzgerald and L. M. White, *The Tabula of Cebes*, SBLTT 24 (Chico, Calif.: Scholars Press, 1983), 144, and cf. J. Behm, "Noeō, etc.," *TDNT* 4 (1967): 976–80; P. Hadot, "Epistrophè et metanoia dans l'histoire de la philosophie," in *Actes du 11 Congrès international de Philosophie* (Brussels, 1953), 12:31–36; R. Joly, "Note sur *metanoia*," *RHR* 160 (1961): 149–56.

90. For further discussion of the terms describing conversion, see Nock, "Conversion and Adolescence" (n. 82 above) and "Bekehrung," *RAC* 2 (1954): 107–8; J. Weiss, *Earliest Christianity: A History of the Period A.D. 30–150*, trans. and ed. F. C. Grant (reprint, New York: Harper & Bros., 1957), 1:233–35. On forsaking home and country: Lucian *Philosophies for Sale* 9. On changing one's profession: Diogenes Laertius *Lives of Eminent Philosophers* 2.125; 3.5; 4.47, on which see J. F. Kindstrand, *Bion of Borysthenes: A Collection of the Fragments with Introduction and Commentary*, Studia Graeca Upsaliensia 11 (Uppsala: Almqvist & Wiksell, 1976), 182.

mixed emotions experienced, are illustrated by the following two examples.[91] In the first, Lucian describes the conversion of someone, perhaps himself,[92] by the philosopher Nigrinus. The speaker in this dialogue had traveled to Rome for medical treatment of the eyes and had gone to Nigrinus's house to pay his respects. He describes how Nigrinus's speech had affected him:

> Beginning to talk on these topics and to explain his position, my dear fellow, he poured enough ambrosial speech over me to put out of date the famous Sirens (if there ever were any) and the nightingales and the lotus of Homer. A divine utterance! For he went on to praise philosophy and the freedom it gives, and to ridicule the things that are popularly considered blessings—wealth and reputation, dominion and honour, yes and purple and gold—things accounted very desirable by most men, and till then by me also. I took it all in with eager, wide-open soul, and at the moment I couldn't imagine what had come over me; I was all confused. At first I felt hurt because he had criticised what was dearest to me—wealth and money and reputation,—and I all but cried over their downfall; and then I thought them paltry and ridiculous, and was glad to be looking up, as it were, out of the murky atmosphere of my past life to a clear sky and great light. In consequence, I actually forgot about my eye and its ailment—would you believe it?—and by degrees grew sharper-sighted in my soul; which, all unawares, I had been carrying about in a purblind condition till then. I went on and on, and so got into the state with which you just now reproached me.
>
> (Lucian *Nigrinus* 3–5)

A second, better-known example of conversion, frequently mentioned in antiquity,[93] is that of Polemo, who in an alcoholic fog stumbled into the room of Xenocrates the philosopher. Although his attitude toward the philosopher is quite different from that of Nigrinus's auditor, the effect of the speech is similar. The speaker is "Philosophy":

---

91. For insights from the psychology of religion, see L. Rambo, "Current Research on Religious Conversion," *RSR* 8 (1982): 145–59; B. R. Gaventa, *From Darkness to Light: Aspects of Conversion in the New Testament,* Overtures to Biblical Theology 20 (Philadelphia: Fortress Press, 1986), 4–8.

92. W. Schmid and O. Stählin, *Geschichte der griechischen Literatur* 2/2, 6th ed. (Munich: Beck, 1920), 712–13.

93. Cf., e.g., Horace *Satire* 2.3.253–57; Epictetus *Discourses* 3.1.14; 4.11.30; Diogenes Laertius *Lives of Eminent Philosophers* 4.16.

But when he came to my house, it chanced that, as usual, the doors were wide open and I was discoursing about virtue and temperance to such of my friends as were there. Coming in upon us with his flute and garlands, first of all he began to shout and tried to break up our meeting by disturbing it with his noise. But we paid no attention to him, and as he was not entirely sodden with Intemperance, little by little he grew sober under the influence of our discourses, took off his garlands, silenced his flute-player, became ashamed of his purple mantle, and, awaking, as it were, from profound sleep, saw his own condition and condemned his past life. The flush that came from Intemperance faded and vanished, and he flushed for shame at what he was doing. At length he abandoned her then and there, and took up with me, not because I either invited or constrained him . . . but voluntarily, because he believed the conditions here were better.

(Lucian The Double Indictment 17)

These two conversions did not take place in a workshop; nevertheless the settings in which they occurred were private or semiprivate, as that provided by Paul's host would have been. They are therefore evidence of how conversion was thought to have been brought about in such settings. The technique of a philosopher, too, is important for our understanding of Paul's method. Persons who heard the moral philosophers were "doing the thing most nearly equivalent to hearing a Christian sermon later: the technique was in fact inherited."[94]

## THE CONVERSION OF THE THESSALONIANS

In the New Testament, conversion is generally described as a response to preaching, sudden, and possibly emotional and dramatic.[95] Some of the terms used to describe conversion to philosophy—for

---

94. Nock, *Conversion,* 177. Nock refers to declamations on virtue and vice, and his statement may have in mind later Christian homilies, but it is equally true of Paul's preaching.

95. For conversion as a response to preaching, our main source is Acts: e.g., 2:41; 14:18; 16:14; 17:4, 11–12; cf. Rom. 10:8–13, 17; 1 Pet. 1:22–25. For a person's dire circumstances bringing him to his senses, see Luke 15:14–19. Paul's conversion or call is extraordinary. For sudden conversions, see Acts 13:42–43, 48; 16:14–15, 29–33; 17:2–4, 10–11; 22:6–10; cf. Luke 19:1–8. Agrippa's words, "So rapidly would you persuade me to become a Christian!" (Acts 26:28), reflect criticism of the phenomenon. See Malherbe, "'Not in a Corner': Early Christian Apologetic in Acts 26:26," *The Second Century* 5 (1986), nn. 76–83. For emotional response, see Acts 2:37. Dramatic: Acts 10:44–45; 14:11–19; cf. Plutarch *Reply to Colotes* 1117B.

example, turning, repentance, and rebirth—are also used of Christian conversion, without necessarily meaning the same thing.[96] So, too, Christian preaching aiming at conversion addressed the sinful human condition and resulted in a confession.[97] These similarities should not be pressed too far; they do, however, demonstrate that conversion was a well-known phenomenon and that Christians used the same language as the philosophers to speak about it.[98]

Paul provides some information on how he expected people to respond positively to his missionary preaching.[99] Faith was to be engendered in their hearts through preaching (Rom. 10:8–10) and oral confession made through the Holy Spirit (1 Cor. 12:3). Like the philosophers, he distinguishes his speech from that of the sophists but does so on the basis of its content, his demeanor and lack of eloquence, and the activity of the Spirit (1 Cor. 2:1–5; cf. 2 Cor. 10:10; 11:6).[100] The Spirit at conversion sanctifies the converts (1 Cor. 6:11; cf. 2 Thess. 2:13), takes up residence in the new believers (Rom. 8:11; Gal. 3:2), and turns their moral lives into religious ones (1 Cor. 6:18–20 cf. 3:17).

This is what transpired in Thessalonica. Like the philosophers, Paul claims to have been emboldened (*eparrēsiasametha*) to speak (1 Thess. 2:1–2), but he also stresses the action of God. God had been active in the conversion of Paul's listeners, for Paul's preaching had taken place with power and the Holy Spirit, had resulted in firm conviction, and had been accepted with great distress mixed with joy inspired by the Spirit (1 Thess. 1:4–6). God gave the believers the Spirit, which was to sanctify their lives (1 Thess. 4:3–8), and they are urged to wake up and be sober (5:6; cf. Rom. 13:1; 1 Cor. 15:34). The speech that led to conversion, unlike that of the philosophers, was

96. Turning (*epistrephein, epistrophē*): Acts 3:19; 9:35; 14:15; 15:3, 19; 1 Pet. 2:25. The "turning" is a turning to God, not a coming to one's senses as with the philosophers. Repentance (*metanoeō, metanoia*): Acts 3:19; 17:30. For a comparison with the pagan use, see A. Oepke, *Die Missionspredigt des Apostels Paulus*, Missionswissenschaftliche Forschungen 2 (Leipzig: Henrichs, 1920), 96–108. Rebirth: James 1:18; 1 Pet. 1:22–23; cf. Titus 3:5.

97. See R. Bultmann, *Theology of the New Testament*, trans. K. Grobel, 2 vols. (New York: Charles Scribner's Sons, 1951), 1:133–37.

98. See Weiss, *Earliest Christianity* (n. 90 above), 1:233–57.

99. See Oepke, *Die Missionspredigt*, 200–211.

100. For the sophistic background of his language in 1 Cor. 2:1–5, see J. Munck, *Paul and the Salvation of Mankind* (Richmond: John Knox Press, 1959), 162–63.

thus conceived by Paul not as a means of giving instruction or itself bringing about a change but as "a means of preparing the way for the supernatural working of God."[101] Summarized thus, and in the light of his statements on the foolishness of his message (1 Cor. 1:21) and his conquering of intellectual fortifications (2 Cor. 10:1–6),[102] the conversions resulting from Paul's preaching may seem to have had only the slightest similarity to their philosophic counterparts. It should be recognized, however, that in these statements Paul reflects theologically, often in polemic or apologetic, on the significance of what had occurred. These statements do not furnish insights into the methods he used in his preaching.

Some information of interest can be extracted from the sermons Paul preached to Gentiles. The outline of a typical Pauline sermon is widely thought to be preserved in 1 Thess. 1:9–10.[103] This message, which began with the knowledge of God (cf. 1 Thess. 4:5), demanded a radical reorientation of outlook and life, exclusive allegiance to God the creator, acceptance of Christ's resurrection, and expectation that Christ would deliver believers from eschatological judgment. The acceptance of the message, as in philosophic conversion, would require a transformation of the mind that would begin at conversion and need constant cultivation (Rom. 12:2).[104] Such Christian preaching to Gentiles, which spoke to the emotion as well as the reason of the hearers, was taken over from Hellenistic-Jewish propaganda which had already appropriated popular philosophic thought.[105]

101. Weiss, *Earliest Christianity* (n. 90 above), 1:250. G. Bornkamm (*Early Christian Experience*, trans. P. L. Hammer [New York: Harper & Row, 1969], 41) holds that reason does not only prepare for the proclamation of the gospel but it "carries through where Paul develops the gospel itself."

102. For the philosophic traditions used in 2 Cor. 10:1–6, see Malherbe, "Antisthenes and Odysseus, and Paul at War," *HTR* 76 (1983): 143–73.

103. P.-E. Langevin, *Jésus Seigneur et l'eschatologie. Exégèse de textes prepauliniens* (Paris: Desclée et Brouwer, 1967), 64–99; G. Schneider, "Urchristliche Gottesverkündigung in hellenistischer Umwelt," *BZ* 13 (1969): 59–75; U. Wilckens, *Die Missionsreden der Apostelgeschichte. Form- und traditionsgeschichtliche Untersuchungen,* WMANT 5 (Neukirchen-Vluyn: Neukirchener Verlag, 1974), 80–86; but see J. Munck, "I Thess. 1.9–10 and the Missionary Preaching of Paul," *NTS* 9 (1962–63): 95–110; G. Friedrich, "Ein Tauflied hellenistischer Judenchristen, 1 Thess. 1, 9f.," *TZ* 21 (1965): 502–16. See also Acts 14:15–17; 17:22–31.

104. See Weiss, *Earliest Christianity,* 1:252–53.

105. See P. Dalbert, *Die Theologie der hellenistisch-jüdischen Missionsliteratur unter Ausschluss von Philo und Josephus* (Hamburg-Volksdorf: Herbert Reich, 1954);

Paul's argument in Romans 1 and 2 is also indebted to these sources, and since it is more extensive than the outline in 1 Thessalonians, it enables us to determine the method of approach Paul likely had used in Thessalonica.[106] Hellenistic-Jewish propaganda made use of Stoic reflection on knowledge of the divine. According to the Stoics, all people have an innate capacity to know God, which must be developed through reason. Falling short of that knowledge means that one is still in ignorance. Since man shares in the essence of the divine, when he attains knowledge of God he comes to a knowledge of himself.[107] The Wisdom of Solomon, especially in chapters 13 and 14, appropriates such thinking in its goal to awaken knowledge of God and dispel ignorance. According to Wisdom of Solomon, it is possible to know God from his works, but people have failed to ascend to that knowledge and have ended in ignorance, which is manifested in idolatry and immorality (cf. Wisd. of Sol. 14:12). They cannot be excused (13:9-10).

Unlike the Stoics and the author of Wisdom, Paul does not take into consideration the innate capacity to know God or the development of divine knowledge through reason. Nevertheless his own use of reason, especially in his missionary preaching, has been insufficiently appreciated.[108] He begins his argument by affirming that God has revealed himself but that the knowledge of God was not appropriated in people's lives (Rom. 1:19, 25, 28), a point he underscores by using vice lists, in the manner of the moral philosophers, to depict

B. Gaertner, *The Areopagus Speech and Natural Revelation*, ASNU 21 (Uppsala: Almqvist & Wiksell, 1955); C. Bussmann, *Themen der paulinischen Missionspredigt auf dem Hintergrund der spätjüdisch-hellenistischen Missionsliteratur* (Bern: Herbert Lang, 1971).

106. See E. Weber, *Die Beziehungen von Röm. 1-3 zur Missionspraxis des Paulus*, BFCT 9:4 (Gütersloh: Bertelsmann, 1905); H. Daxer, *Römer 1, 18—2, 10 im Verhältnis zur spätjüdischen Lehrauffassung* (Diss.; Naumburg: Pätz, 1914); Bornkamm, *Early Christian Experience*, 47-70.

107. For an interpretation of the Stoic view, see Gaertner, *The Areopagus Speech*, 105-16.

108. D. W. Kemmler (*Faith and Human Reason: A Study of Paul's Method of Preaching as Illustrated by 1-2 Thessalonians and Acts 17, 2-4*, NovTSup 40 [Leiden: E. J. Brill, 1975]) is one-sided and uncritically dependent on Acts. The best treatment is Bornkamm, *Early Christian Experience* (n. 101 above), 1-70. For a comparison of Romans with early Christian apologetic, see A. J. Malherbe, "The Apologetic Theology of the Preaching of Peter," *Restoration Quarterly* 13 (1970): 205-23.

the human condition (Rom. 1:24–32). This condition is due not to ignorance but to willfulness (1:23, 25) and shows man to be without excuse (1:20; 2:1, cf. 15) and deserving of God's judgment (2:2, 5–10). God's kindness, however, provides man with an opportunity to repent (2:4) and escape that judgment when God, through Christ, lays bare the human condition with its conflicts (2:15–16).[109] The argument is vehement, as Paul's sermon would have been, in its thrust to convict rather than to inform. Paul's aim to create conflict in his readers and convict them of their sinful condition is similar to that of the philosophers.

While the speech is rational, the response Paul envisaged is also similar to philosophic conversion in that it involved the total person. The clearest statement in Paul's letters about the desired effect on a non-Christian of intelligible or rational speech, in this case the speech of Christian prophets, is 1 Cor. 14:24–25:

> But if all prophesy, and an unbeliever or outsider enters, he is convicted by all, he is called to account by all, the secrets of his heart are disclosed; and so, falling on his face, he will worship God and declare that God is really among you.[110]

Paul's description of the Thessalonians as having received the word with deep distress (RSV: "much affliction") combined with joy (1 Thess. 1:6) shows that, like the converts to philosophy, his converts had responded with profoundly mixed emotions.[111]

The similarities between Paul and the philosophers should not be pressed too far. Closer examination reveals significant differences, in addition to those already noted. The content of his preaching, particularly such items as the resurrection of Christ and eschatological

109. For this use of repentance, rare in Paul, see Weiss, *Earliest Christianity,* 1:252-3.

110. Bornkamm (*Early Christian Experience,* 39) compares the passage with Rom. 2:14–15 and comments: "The term 'convict' seems to me especially characteristic, for its primary and intrinsic meaning is not to become theoretically convinced of the correctness of a doctrine. Rather, it aims at the man himself who hears the word, that confronted by the truth and reality of this word, his inner being may be revealed."

111. See the discussion in chap. 2 of the "afflictions" of the converts. For the "enthusiasm" with which Paul is thought to have preached and with which his message is thought to have been received, see Weinel, *St. Paul,* 206; cf. D. J. Lull, *The Spirit in Galatia: Paul's Interpretation of Pneuma as Divine Power,* SBLDS 49 (Chico, Calif.: Scholars Press, 1980), 52–95, but note the contrary viewpoint in Warneck, *Paulus,* 117–19; Oepke, *Die Missionspredigt* (n. 96 above), 117–19.

judgment, was manifestly different. Of major significance is that, whereas the philosophers stressed the importance of reason and reliance on self in moral growth, Paul refers the moral life to God and the power of the Holy Spirit. The philosophers, furthermore, through character education aimed at virtue and happiness, for the attainment of which one could be justly proud. Paul, on the other hand, while he does speak of a transformation, as the philosophers do, has in mind a metamorphosis of the intellect that rejects conformity to the world and aims at discerning the will of God (Rom. 12:1–2). For him the goal is not the achievement of one's natural potential but the formation of Christ in the believer (Gal. 4:19; cf. Rom. 8:29). Despite such differences, however, the similarities are obvious and are the more striking in light of the way Paul makes use of moral philosophic traditions throughout 1 Thessalonians.[112]

This chapter has focused on the setting in which Paul preached in Thessalonica and on the manner in which he brought individuals to conversion, thus founding the church. In the semiprivate setting of a workshop, plying his trade in the company of fellow manual laborers, he proclaimed the knowledge of God in a manner that revealed to his listeners their own condition and that turned them to God. It now remains for us to examine how Paul shaped a community out of these individuals.

112. See Malherbe, "Exhortation in First Thessalonians," *NovT* 25 (1983): 238–56. Cf. J. N. Sevenster, "Education or Conversion: Epictetus and the Gospels," *NovT* 8 (1966): 247–62, who tends to overstress the differences between Stoic philosophy and Christianity.

# 2
# Shaping the Community

## CHURCHES AS COMMUNITIES

Recent sociological studies have drawn attention to Paul's churches as communities. Once it is recognized that these small groups were highly stratified socially, representing a considerable cross section of Roman society, Paul's treatment of the points at issue in them takes on new light, as several writers have demonstrated.[1] Such sociological studies compare Paul's churches with other ancient groups—the household, voluntary associations, the synagogue, and philosophical and rhetorical schools—and with the aid of social theory suggest reasons why Christianity attracted converts.[2] Two sometimes related factors are seen to have been at work. The converts, particularly those in some of Paul's churches, were upwardly mobile and had achieved higher social status than that attributed to them by society. Wayne Meeks queries whether Christianity may have had characteristics that were particularly attractive to persons of high "status inconsistency." One such characteristic, Meeks suggests, may have been the intimacy of the Christian groups, which provided welcome refuge from the loneliness accompanying

1. Theissen, *Social Setting* (chap. 1, n. 11), 69–119; Meeks, *First Urban Christians,* 51–73; Malherbe, *Social Aspects,* 60–91, 118–21.
2. See Meeks, *First Urban Christians,* 75–84, on the different groups. For the reasons that people converted to Christianity, see R. Scroggs, "The Earliest Christian Communities as Sectarian Movement," in *Christianity, Judaism and Other Greco-Roman Cults: Studies for Morton Smith at Sixty,* ed. J. Neusner, 4 vols. (Leiden: E. J. Brill, 1975), 2:1–23; J. G. Gager, *Kingdom and Community: The Social World of Early Christianity* (Englewood Cliffs, N.J.: Prentice-Hall, 1975), esp. 19–49.

status inconsistency.[3] Indeed, the view that a sense of loneliness or deprivation caused potential converts to seek out the community offered by the Christian groups is not uncommon.[4]

An earlier description of the church by Wilhelm Bousset, which would be modified considerably by contemporary scholars engaged in sociological inquiry, nevertheless reflects in part a similar understanding of the social factors involved:

> Here in the gatherings of the fellowship, in worship and cult, there grew up for the believers in Christ the consciousness of their unity and peculiar sociological exclusiveness. During the day scattered, in the vocations of everyday life, in solitariness, within an alien world abandoned to scorn and contempt, they came together in the evening, probably as often as possible, for the common sacred meal. There they experienced the miracle of fellowship, the glow of the enthusiasm of a common faith and a common hope; there the spirit blazed high, and a world full of wonders surrounded them; prophets and those who speak in tongues, visionaries and ecstatic persons begin to speak; psalms, hymns, and spiritual songs sound through the room, the powers of brotherly kindness come alive in unexpected fashion; an unprecedented new life pulses through the throng of the Christians. And over this whole swaying sea of inspiration reigns the Lord Jesus as the head of his community, with his power immediately present in breathtaking palpable presence and certainty.[5]

But the situation of new converts may have been more complex than is implied by Bousset's romantic description. Such generalizations must be put to the test in particular instances.

3. See Meeks, *First Urban Christians*, 73, 191. Meeks offers this as one among several possible points of appeal of the Christian groups, and he is characteristically cautious in drawing conclusions. For a critique of Meeks, see S. K. Stowers, "The Social Sciences and the Study of Early Christianity," in *Approaches to Ancient Judaism*, vol. 5, *Studies in Judaism and Its Greco-Roman Context*, ed. W. S. Green (Atlanta: Scholars Press, 1985), 149–81, esp. 168–76.

4. See, e.g., Scroggs, "The Earliest Christian Communities" (n. 2 above), 5, 19; J. H. Elliott, *A Home for the Homeless: A Sociological Exegesis of 1 Peter, Its Situation and Strategy* (Philadelphia: Fortress Press, 1981), 77–78; Gager, *Kingdom and Community*, 129–42. For a later period, see A. D. Nock, *Conversion* (chap. 1, n. 30), 211; E. R. Dodds, *Pagan and Christian in an Age of Anxiety* (Cambridge: Cambridge Univ. Press, 1965), 136–38, who is contradicted by P. Brown, *The Making of Late Antiquity* (Cambridge, Mass.: Harvard Univ. Press, 1978), 1–11. For a criticism of theories of deprivation, see White, "Adolf Harnack and the 'Expansion' of Christianity: A Reappraisal of Social History," *The Second Century* 5 (1985/86): 97–127.

5. W. Bousset, *Kyrios Christos: A History of the Belief in Christ from the Beginnings of Christianity to Irenaeus*, trans. J. E. Steely (Nashville: Abingdon Press, 1970), 135.

Our investigation of the founding of the church in Thessalonica discovered Paul performing manual labor and converting other laborers. In this case, there is no evidence that the church was socially stratified to a degree that caused problems calling for Paul's attention. It must be significant, for example, that a person like Jason is not mentioned by Paul. Nor is there any indication that the Thessalonian Christians had achieved high social status before their conversion. In chapter 4 two things will be demonstrated: that some of these Christians sought to change their status *after* their conversion and that Paul claims to have been consistent from his first encounter with them in exhorting them to continue in their achieved roles. In 1 Thessalonians, Paul does strive to foster bonds within the community, in a way suggesting that the fellowship provided by the church was a powerful factor in shaping it. It is nevertheless possible that the description of the church as "refuge" may only obscure the actual experiences of the converts whom Paul had to nurture in a new belief and way of life.

Thus far we have focused on Paul's preaching as the means by which he converted people, not on the features of the Christian communities that may have attracted outsiders. It should be clear that this use of preaching as a means for effecting conversion, as well as his methods for founding churches, had precedents among contemporary philosophers. Now we explore the possibility that Paul's techniques for shaping his converts into a coherent community can be illuminated by comparing them with the procedures that philosophers used in guiding their disciples' moral formation. Such procedures typically took into consideration the psychological and social states of persons who undertook a new way of life in a philosophic or religious community. Therefore it will be helpful to begin with a comparison between the philosophers' procedures in shaping new members of the community and Paul's own techniques by looking at the philosophers' assessments of the conditions of new converts.

## THE CONDITIONS OF NEW CONVERTS

Conversion was a disturbing experience that did not lead to a placid life in a safe harbor. The radical reorientation demanded by philosophers required social, intellectual, and moral transformation that often resulted in confusion, bewilderment, and sometimes dejection. The pedagogic concerns of the philosophic subculture represented by such persons as Epictetus and Plutarch reveal the constant attention that was given to the nurture of those who had embarked on a new way of life.[6] Epictetus conducted a philosophic school for young men preparing to enter public life. Conversions to philosophy frequently occurred among the young, and Epictetus's harsh comments show us the conflicts that raged in his students.[7] Plutarch, on the other hand, does not primarily have the young in mind, but since his concerns are partly similar to those of Epictetus, it is reasonable to take the comments of both as reflecting the problems of neophytes in philosophy irrespective of their age.[8] Allowance should of course be made for individual circumstances and perhaps for the sharpness with which the young might define their options and experience the lures of the nonphilosophic life. It will suffice, however, to identify what appears to have been typical.

Epictetus constantly had to deal with the despair of his students as they faced the new life. His words are surprisingly severe:

> You sit trembling for fear that something will happen, and lamenting, and grieving, and groaning about other things that are happening. . . . Although you have these faculties free and entirely your own, you do not use them, nor do you realize what gifts you have received, and from whom, but you sit sorrowing and groaning, some of you blinded toward the giver himself and not even acknowledging your benefactor, and others,—such is their ignoble spirit—turning aside to fault-finding and complaints against God.
>
> (Epictetus *Discourse* 1.6.38, 41–42)

Peevishly he accuses them of not having made a clean break with their past and of finding fault with him:

6. The best general treatment is still P. Rabbow, *Seelenführung. Methodik der Exerzitien in der Antike* (Munich: Kösel-Verlag, 1954). See also P. Hadot, *Exercices spirituels et philosophie antique* (Paris: Études Augustiniennes, 1981), 13–70, esp. for bibliography.

7. On Epictetus's school, see T. Colardeau, *Étude sur Épictète* (Paris: Fontemoing, 1903), 71–206; O. Halbauer, *De diatribis Epicteti* (Leipzig: Bornen, 1911), 43–56; J. Souilhé, *Épictète: Entretiens* (Paris: Association Budé, 1943), xxx–xlii; and esp. Hijmans, *ASKESIS* (chap. 1, n. 60).

8. On the school setting of Plutarch's works, see Schmid and Stählin, *Geschichte der griechischen Literatur* (chap. 1, n. 92), 2/1, 489; K. Ziegler, "Plutarchos," PW 21 (1951): 662–65; R. H. Barrow, *Plutarch and His Times* (London: Chatto & Windus, 1967), 72–118.

You go back to the same things again; you have exactly the same desires as before, the same aversions, in the same way you make your choices, your designs, and your purposes, you pray for the same things and are interested in the same things. In the second place, you do not even look for anybody to give you advice, but you are annoyed if you are told what I am telling you. Again, you say, "He is an old man without the milk of human kindness in him."[9]

(Epictetus *Discourse* 2.17.36–38)

From Epictetus's cutting words one can infer the causes of his students' grief and despair. An assuming of the philosophic life implied abandoning one's comrades, haunts, and customary social relationships. Epictetus might compare the aspirant philosopher to a little child crying for his nurse and mother, but his sarcasm only throws into sharper relief the turmoil of his students. That their decisions caused grief to those they had left did not ease their own anxiety.[10]

The philosophers-to-be were acutely aware of public opinion and were embarrassed by it. Epictetus's description of such opinion is to the point:

Yes, but suppose I set the good somewhere here, among the things that the will controls, all men will laugh at me. Some white-haired old man with many a gold ring on his fingers will come along, and then he will shake his head and say, "Listen to me, sonny; one ought of course to philosophize, but one ought also to keep one's head; this is all nonsense. You learn a syllogism from the philosophers, but you know better than the philosophers what you ought to do."

(Epictetus *Discourse* 1.22.18–19)

That they were without honor and were regarded as nobodies depressed (*thlibesthai*) the disciples.[11]

Convinced that in social intercourse one either influences one's associates or is influenced by them, Epictetus feared that his students might be enticed from the philosophic life by people who did not take it seriously; he therefore advised that they not associate with non-philosophers until they themselves were secure in their philosophic

---

9. See Hijmans, *ASKESIS* (chap. 1, n. 60), 100–102; cf. Rabbow, *Seelenführung* (n. 6 above), 263–64; Lucian *Philosophies for Sale* 9.
10. For what is given up, see Epictetus, *Discourse* 2.16.24–47; cf. 2.12.10–14; 3.24.5, 9. For grief caused to others, see *Discourse* 3.24.22.
11. Epictetus *Encheiridion* 24. For *thlipsis* in Epictetus's thought, see H. Schlier, "Thlibō, thlipsis," *TDNT* 3 (1965): 139–40.

formation.[12] The association with persons who held similar values did not, however, allay the students' feeling of loneliness, even desolation, either in the midst of their fellow students or in the larger society.[13]

Plutarch, in his tractate on how to become aware of one's progress in virtue, does not write with a school like Epictetus's in mind. He does, however, provide proof that the conditions and problems of novices to the philosophic life that we have identified were typical. Plutarch vividly sketches the dissatisfaction that the convert to philosophy experiences with ordinary pursuits,[14] but tempers the idealistic picture of the sobriety, clarity, and calm that philosophy brings by stressing the difficulties that are initially encountered.

One of Plutarch's major concerns addressed in this tractate is the disappointment of beginners with the slow progress they were making in the philosophic life. The perplexity, errant thought, and vacillation experienced by beginners contributed to this disappointment.[15] Elsewhere he also speaks of their confusion, hard work, and uncertainty, of the danger of their being crushed and disheartened, and of the temptation to desert philosophy when personal demands are made on them.[16] Furthermore, their strained social relationships could weaken their commitment:

> The sober advice of friends and the bitter criticisms of the unfriendly, in the form of scoffing and joking, cause a warping and weakening of purpose, and have even made some persons renounce philosophy altogether.
>
> (Plutarch *Progress in Virtue* 78A–C)

Plutarch illustrates the alienation and dejection of the philosophic tyro by quoting a well-known anecdote about Diogenes's turning to philosophy:

> The Athenians were keeping holiday with public banquets and shows in the theatre and informal gatherings among themselves, and indulging in merry-making the whole night long, while Diogenes,

12. Epictetus *Discourse* 3.16.
13. See Epictetus *Discourse* 3.13.1–3.
14. Plutarch *Progress in Virtue* 77BC. On this tractate, see W. Grese, "De Profectibus in Virtute (Moralia 75A–86A)," in *Plutarch's Ethical Writings and Early Christian Literature,* SCHNT 4, ed. H. D. Betz (Leiden: E. J. Brill, 1978), 11–31.
15. Plutarch *Progress in Virtue* 77D.
16. Plutarch *On Listening to Lectures* 46E–47B.

huddled up in a corner trying to sleep, fell into some very disturbing and disheartening reflections how he from no compulsion had entered upon a toilsome and strange mode of life, and as a result of his own act he was now sitting without part or parcel in all these good things.

(Plutarch *Progress in Virtue* 77EF)

This loneliness, which we have also encountered in Epictetus, appears to have been experienced by recent converts, regardless of their school affiliation.[17] A Pauline church represented more than the philosophic subculture with which Epictetus and Plutarch were concerned. It was an alternative community which had things in common with the Epicureans. Although he does not himself draw the parallel, Bernard Frischer has recently offered an interpretation of the Epicureans that in many ways is similar to the view of early Christian communities noted above.[18] According to Frischer, the Epicurean communities offered a safe harbor, a home to the uprooted and alienated in a community that provided an appealing alternative to the dominant culture.[19] Epicureanism seems especially to have attracted students of philosophy who were tired of their low status in the eyes of the majority and of the stress brought on by social alienation and intellectual skepticism.[20] Epicurean communities were formed as disciples gathered around Epicurus and later leaders and followed their examples.[21] Epicurus provided security and was addressed as "father," and the social policy of the communities included intermarriage between members of the group; such factors helped to simulate kinship among all the members of the

17. See, e.g., the fragment from a lost play of Menander, translated in Festugière, *Epicurus and His Gods* (chap. 1, n. 88), 39: "I'm alone here; there'll be no one to hear what I'm going to say." For a different interpretation, see K. Gaiser, "Ein Lob Athens in der Komödie (Menander, Fragmentum Didotianum b)," *Gymnasium* 75 (1968): 193–219, and the literature cited there. But see A.-J. Festugière, *La Vie spirituelle in Grèce a l'époque hellénistique* (Paris: A. & J. Picard, n.d.) 157–62.

18. B. Frischer, *The Sculpted Word: Epicureanism and Philosophical Recruitment* (Berkeley and Los Angeles: Univ. of California Press, 1982), 46–66. Cf. Hadot, *Seneca* (chap. 1, n. 60), 49–52.

19. Frischer, *Sculpted Word*, 52, where he distinguishes between a subculture and an alternative community.

20. Frischer, *Sculpted Word*, 65.

21. Frischer, *Sculpted Word*, 124–25, 205–7. Cf. W. Schmid, "Epikur," *RAC* 5 (1962): 745–47, and see Seneca *Epistles* 11.8; 25.5: the disciples are to do everything in the spiritual presence of the master.

group.[22] The Epicureans formed genuine communities, in which they pursued the routine activities of life in addition to studying.[23]

André-Jean Festugière has attributed the long-lasting fascination of Epicureanism to Epicurus's success in founding a new family of friends:

> Sheltered from the world and the buffetings of Fortune, this little group had the feeling that they had reached the harbor. They nestled down together under the protection of the Sage whose words were received as oracles. There was no more need to doubt or to re-examine their problems; Epicurus had solved them once and for all. It was enough to believe, to obey, and to love one another.[24]

This sympathetic, indeed romantic, view of the Epicureans is not unlike Bousset's description of early Christian groups.

It would be a mistake if this idyllic picture of the Epicureans led to the assumption that they did not share the experiences of other converts to philosophy. We do not know as much about the Epicureans' methods of bringing about conversion as we do those of other philosophers; it may be the case that converts to Epicureanism were themselves attracted to the school rather than that they were actively pursued by its members.[25] Nor do we know as much about the Epicureans' psychology of conversion as we do that of the philosophers who have so far come under consideration. Evidence suggests, however, that the psychological states of Epicurean converts—whatever the means by which they were converted—were not materially different from those of converts to other philosophies.

In an attempt to reconstruct the Epicurean theory of conversion, Frischer accepts the social-scientific view of conversion as a radical redefinition of personal identity that "comes about through a dual insight, at once painful and exhilarating, into the inadequacies of the old self, felt to be sick and impoverished, and the path to be taken toward a new self, perceived as more healthy and whole."[26] Frischer

22. Frischer, *Sculpted Word*, 64.
23. Frischer, *Sculpted Word*, 63.
24. Festugière, *Epicurus and His Gods* (chap. 1, n. 88), 41–42.
25. For the two types, see Diogenes Laertius *Lives of Eminent Philosophers* 9.112. Frischer (*Sculpted Word*) argues brilliantly, but not without tendentiousness, for the former.
26. Frischer, *Sculpted Word*, 71–72.

concludes that the crucial step to conversion was a desire to become similar to the Epicurean gods: an act at once self-critical and renewing.[27] The conversion of Colotes, who threw himself down before Epicurus and embraced his knees while Epicurus lectured, would seem to indicate that conversion could indeed be an emotional experience.[28]

The Epicurean communities were highly structured, and as we shall see in chapter 3 their members were assiduous in self-criticism and in exhorting and instructing one another. It was regarded as of the utmost importance that the Epicurean friends be frank (*parrēsiazesthai*) with each other, and the responses to this outspokenness that are described by the philosophers reveal the conditions or states of recent converts.[29] Some of the converts were "tender" and weak.[30] Stung by frankness,[31] they became confused and still weaker because they did not recognize its value.[32] Because they were weak, or because frankness could not cure them, it was always possible that they might desert philosophy[33] or fall into error.[34] Sometimes their relationships with one another caused them pain, and they grieved over their associates' deaths.[35]

In addition to problems of personal growth and intracommunal relationships, the Epicureans experienced difficulties in their

27. Frischer, *Sculpted Word*, 83.

28. Plutarch *Reply to Colotes* 1117B, on which see Festugière, *Epicurus and His Gods* (chap. 1, n. 88), 40–41; R. Westman, *Plutarch gegen Kolotes. Seine Schrift 'Adversus Colotem' als philosophiegeschichtliche Quelle*, APFenn 7 (Helsinki: Akateeminen Kirjakauppa, 1955), 27–31.

29. Our major source is Philodemus *On Frankness* (*Peri Parrēsias*). The text cited is A. Olivieri, *Philodemi Peri Parrēsias* (Leipzig: Teubner, 1914). See also Plutarch *How to Tell a Flatterer from a Friend*, which concludes with a discussion of frankness (59A–74E) that has much in common with Philodemus's tractate. I am thankful to David Fredrickson for assistance in trying to understand Philodemus.

30. Philodemus *On Frankness* 7a; cf. Tab. III G.

31. Philodemus *On Frankness* XVIIb.

32. Philodemus *On Frankness* IV, XVIIb; cf. XXIa.

33. Philodemus *On Frankness* 59; cf. IX.

34. Philodemus *On Frankness* 35; cf. IX.

35. See Philodemus *On Frankness* 61; XV, for grief in personal relationships. See Plutarch *That Epicurus Actually Makes a Pleasant Life Impossible* 1101AB, for their reputation of being softhearted because they grieved at someone's death. For Epicurus's and his followers' letters of consolation, see D. Clay, "Individual and Community in the First Generation of the Epicurean School, *SYZETESIS: Studi sull' epicureismo greco e romano offerti a Marcello Gigante*, Biblioteca della Parola del Passato 16 (Naples: Gaetano Macchiaroli, 1983), 266–69.

relationships with the larger society. In theory, their communities, to which they withdrew from public life, provided them with security.[36] Convinced that security was not derived from being famous, they were not to engage in political activity[37] and would not conform to popular opinion to win praise from the masses.[38] Social criticism of the Epicureans was severe, sometimes claiming that their quietism was a threat to the state.[39] More to the point for our purpose, their opponents claimed that living the good life required participation in society, and they attacked the Epicureans' honesty.[40] Plutarch, for example, charged that the Epicureans in fact did love praise and fame but that it was because of their lack of ability that they shunned public life. To be held in low esteem, Plutarch claimed, is painful, and nothing is held in lower esteem than to be without friends, inactive, atheistic, sensual, and indifferent, which was the "esteem" in which Epicureans were held.[41] Despite their protestations to the contrary, some members of the Epicurean communities were indeed sensitive to the social tensions caused by their new way of life. Zeno of Sidon spoke on the low opinion of them held by the masses and on their separation from their families,[42] and there is evidence that, like Epictetus's disciples, the Epicureans too were vexed and distressed (*thlibontai*) by being without respect.[43] Thus it appears that the condition of Epicurean converts was, in important respects, similar to that of other converts to philosophy.

Another group that illustrate the difficulties experienced, in this case by converts to a minority religion, were the proselytes to

36. Epicurus *Principal Doctrines* 14. See Schmid, "Epikur," *RAC* 5 (1962): 723–26; H. C. Baldry, *The Unity of Mankind in Greek Thought* (Cambridge: Cambridge Univ. Press, 1965), 147–50; Festugière, *Epicurus and His Gods* (chap. 1, n. 88), 27–50; Frischer, *Sculpted Word* (n. 18 above), 75–76.

37. Philodemus *On Frankness* 7; Vatican Collection 58; Diogenes Laertius *Lives of Eminent Philosophers* 10.119. Some, however, did; see Frischer, *Sculpted Word*, 75 n. 21.

38. Vatican Collection 29.

39. E.g., Plutarch *Reply to Colotes* 1125C. This was a polemical overstatement. See Schmid, "Epikur" (n. 36 above), 727–30.

40. E.g., Plutarch *Reply to Colotes* 1108C.

41. Plutarch *That Epicurus Actually Makes a Pleasant Life Impossible* 1100BC; cf. *Is 'Live Unknown' a Wise Precept?* 1128A–C, 1129A–D, 1130E.

42. Philodemus *On Frankness* 3.

43. Philodemus *On Frankness* XXIIa.

Judaism.[44] Although they were frequently said to have found shelter or refuge in Judaism,[45] their entrance into that religion was a radical experience. As part of a rite of admission, the proselyte was asked, "Do you not know that in these times the Israelites are afflicted, distressed, downtrodden, torn to pieces, and that suffering is their lot?"[46] The break with their past was signified by their being called newborn children.[47] Attitudes toward proselytes differed from teacher to teacher and circumstance to circumstance, so that a proselyte could not always be assured of a cordial reception.[48] On the pagan side, the attitude is well described by Tacitus: "The earliest lesson they receive is to despise the gods, to disown their country, and to regard their parents, children, and brothers as of little account."[49] It is natural that abandoning so much could cause proselytes to feel alienated and forlorn, a condition described poignantly in a prayer by Asenath, a proselyte:

> Preserve me, Lord, for I am desolate, for my father and my mother have renounced me, because I destroyed and crushed their gods, and now I am an orphan and desolate. I have no other hope but in Thee, Lord, for thou art the father of orphans, the protector of the persecuted, and helper of the distressed (*thlibomenōn*). . . . Look upon my orphan state, Lord, for I have fled to Thee."[50]
>
> (*Joseph and Asenath* 12.11; 13.1)

The texts just quoted from are later, some considerably later, than Paul. Philo's description of how proselytes should be treated, however, shows that these conditions already obtained in the first century. Philo considers it necessary to encourage his readers to give special

---

44. For much of what follows, see E. Pax, "Beobachtungen zur Konvertitensprache im ersten Thessalonicherbrief," *Studii Biblici Franciscani Analecta* 21 (1971): 220–61, and "Konvertitenprobleme im ersten Thessalonicherbrief," *Bibel und Leben* 13 (1972): 24–37.

45. G. F. Moore, *Judaism in the First Centuries of the Christian Era*, 3 vols. (Cambridge, Mass.: Harvard Univ. Press, 1927), 1:330.

46. *Yebamoth* 47ab. This was after the war under Hadrian, but the rite of which this was part may predate the fall of Jerusalem. Cf. Moore, *Judaism*, 3:109–10.

47. Primarily to describe their legal status. See Moore, *Judaism* (n. 45 above), 1:334–45; K. G. Kuhn, "Prosēlytos," *TDNT* 6 (1968), 739–40; J. Jeremias, *Jerusalem in the Time of Jesus*, trans. F. H. and C. H. Cave (Philadelphia: Fortress Press, 1969), 324–25.

48. See Moore, *Judaism*, 1:341–48; Kuhn, "Prosēlytos," *TDNT* 6 (1968), 737–38.

49. Tacitus *Histories* 5.5.

50. On the *thlipsis* of the proselyte, see further Pax, "Beobachtungen" (n. 44 above), 240–41.

attention to proselytes. He thinks that they, like widows and orphans, are weak and lowly.[51] In justifying his appeal for benevolent concern, Philo details what the proselytes have left by coming to a new refuge:[52] friends, kinfolk of whom they have made mortal enemies, country, ancestral gods, and honors. Philo further emphasizes the proselytes' alienation from their former lives by describing them as deserters, migrants, pilgrims, and persons who have abandoned their former relationships.[53] Such persons are to be honored with respect, special friendship, and more than ordinary goodwill and are to be provided with other cities, family relations, and friends.[54] Jews should

> love the incomers, not only as friends and kinsfolk but as themselves both in body and soul: in bodily matters, by acting as far as may be for the common interest; in mental by having the same griefs and joys, so that they may seem to be the separate parts of a single living being which is compacted and unified by their fellowship in it.
>
> (Philo *On Virtues* 103)

In addition, the Jews should provide proselytes with food, drink, clothing, and other daily needs, for all these things are required by the law, which speaks "of the friendliness shown by him who loves the incomer even as himself."[55] Such directions presuppose the conditions of new converts we have identified.

In sum, it appears that, regardless of what attraction a cult or philosophical sect might have exercised, conversion brought with it social as well as religious and intellectual dislocation, which in turn created confusion, bewilderment, dejection, and even despair in the converts. An emphasis on the newness of the convert's experience and standing might be accompanied by discouragement at the slow progress in the new life. This distress was increased by the break with the ancestral religion and mores, with family, friends, and associates, and by public criticism. The groups considered here took special care to assimilate new members and foster their personal development. The special identity and nature of the new community was

51. Philo *Special Laws* 4.177; *On Dreams* 2.273.
52. Philo *Special Laws* 1.52; *On Dreams* 2.273.
53. Philo *Special Laws* 1.51–53; 4.178; *On Virtues* 102.
54. Philo *Special Laws* 1.52; cf. *On Virtues* 103–4, 179.
55. Philo *On Virtues* 104.

accentuated in a number of ways. The relationship between the community and the larger society was clarified, and within the community the language of kinship was used to describe the new communal reality. God, or in the case of the Epicureans the founder of the community, was viewed as father, and the members as children and siblings. New members especially were described as children. Epictetus does so chidingly, when he compares distressed students to little children who long for their nurses and mothers. Proselytes described themselves as desolate orphans who looked to God as their father.

## THE THESSALONIAN CONVERTS

Paul's converts apparently experienced the same distress and anxiety at and after their conversion that converts to other groups experienced. Here we are concerned with Paul's initial shaping of the community, with his special interest in his converts' psychological state and their social relationships. Although our only source is 1 Thessalonians, which was written months after the original molding of the community, it nevertheless provides us with some relevant information.

In Paul's first reference to the Thessalonians' conversion, he writes that they had "received the word in much affliction (*thlipsis*), with joy inspired by the Holy Spirit" (1:6). He returns to the subject of affliction in 3:3–4, 7, where he recounts the circumstances that led to the writing of the letter. The meaning of *thlipsis* and its verbal cognate in these passages is not immediately clear. *Thlipsis* is used figuratively here but whether of external oppression, such as persecution, or of internal distress is not obvious. The majority of commentators decide for the former and refer to 2:14 and Acts 17:5–9 (cf. 1 Thess. 2:2) to identify the persecutors.[56] This removes from *thlipsis* in 1:6 any reference to the psychological state of the converts. As Ernest Best puts it, "Indeed, inward anxieties are actually absent for the outward tribulations are received with joy of the Holy Spirit."[57]

56. E.g., J. E. Frame, *The Epistles of St. Paul to the Thessalonians*, ICC (Edinburgh: T. & T. Clark, 1912), 82–83; F. F. Bruce, *1 & 2 Thessalonians*, WBC (Waco, Tex.: Word Publishers, 1982), 15–16; Donfried, "The Cults of Thessalonica and the Thessalonian Correspondence," *NTS* 31 (1985): 347, 349–50.

57. E. Best, *A Commentary on the First and Second Epistles to the Thessalonians*, HNTC (New York: Harper & Row, 1972), 79.

Another interpretation relativizes the distress of the Thessalonians. Howard Marshall, for example, thinks that Paul's specific reference is to persecution but that the principle that Christian joy allows the believer to bear suffering "applies to all the other pains and irritations which can fill the attention of the non-believer but which are of trivial importance to the believer."[58] Viewed thus, the afflictions are further understood by some commentators in the light of the Jewish notion of the eschatological sufferings of the righteous.[59]

Such interpretations, however, are not satisfactory. Paul relates his converts' *thlipsis* to their reception of the gospel and not to persecution they might have experienced later, especially after he had left Thessalonica. Furthermore, their persecutions were at the hands of their countrymen (2:14), presumably non-Jews, and can therefore not be identified with the events described in Acts 17:5-9. Nor can Paul's comments on his own experiences after his founding of the church be pressed into support of this interpretation. If 1 Thess. 2:15 does refer to Paul's ejection from Thessalonica, it obviously occurred after the Thessalonians' conversion and does not contribute to our understanding of *thlipsis* in 1:6.

It is possible that Paul's reference to the "great opposition (*agōn*)" that he faced in Thessalonica after he had suffered in Philippi (2:2) will bring his own experience into closer relation to that of the Thessalonians when he boldly preached the gospel to them. Many commentators understand *agōn* to refer to external dangers that Paul faced, while some understand it to refer to the anxiety with which he preached.[60] John Chrysostom's view that Paul had both in mind may be closer to the truth.[61]

---

58. I. H. Marshall, *1 and 2 Thessalonians*, NCB (Grand Rapids: Wm. B. Eerdmans, 1983), 54.

59. See Schlier, "Thlibō, thlipsis," *TDNT* 3 (1965): 144–48; R. F. Collins, *Studies on the First Letter to the Thessalonians*, BETL 66 (Leuven-Louvain: Univ. Press, 1984), 191–93, 291–93.

60. External: G. Milligan, *St. Paul's Epistles to the Thessalonians* (London: Macmillan, 1908), 17; Best, *Commentary* (n. 57 above), 91–92; Bruce, *1 & 2 Thessalonians* (n. 56 above), 25. Anxiety: E. von Dobschütz, *Die Thessalonicherbriefe*, KEK (Göttingen: Vandenhoeck & Ruprecht, 1909), 85; Frame, *Epistles of St. Paul* (n. 56 above), 94; B. Rigaux, *Saint Paul: Les Épîtres aux Thessaloniciens*, EB (Paris: Gabalda: 1956), 405.

61. John Chrysostom *Homilies on First Thessalonians*, *Homily* 2 (PG 62:401); cf. W. Neil, *The Epistle of Paul to the Thessalonians*, MNTC (London: Hodder & Stoughton, 1950), 35.

Paul refers to his *agōn* at the beginning of a description of his work in Thessalonica that is heavily indebted to descriptions of the ideal philosopher (1 Thess. 2:1–12). In such descriptions, the Stoic and Cynic sage is the moral athlete whose *agōn* may be with immoral men but is preeminently a struggle with his own passions and emotions as he fulfills his purpose in the natural scheme of things.[62] Paul's self-description in 1 Thess. 2:1–6 stresses the divine purpose and Paul's own motivation and integrity, thus indicating that it was primarily an inward struggle that he had in mind. Engaged in such a struggle, he preached to the Thessalonians, and some of them became imitators of him by accepting his unsettling message with a mixture of distress and joy. It has already been shown that recent converts spoke of their distress and that mixed emotions were characteristic of conversion. In view of the preceding analysis, then, it is reasonable to understand *thlipsis* in 1:6 as the distress and anguish of heart experienced by persons who broke with their past as they received the gospel.[63] Like other converts, these new Christians in Thessalonica continued to be distressed, and they needed encouragement and instruction lest they be tempted to abandon the faith (3:3–4).

It is likely that Paul's concentrated use of kinship language in 1 Thessalonians also points to a problem his readers faced after their conversion. In the letter, God is called the "father" of Jesus Christ (1:10; 1:1?), and three times "our Father" (1:3; 3:11, 13). Paul, in addition to being their "father" (2:11), is also an "orphan" (2:17; RSV: "bereft") and a "nurse" (2:7), and the Thessalonians are his "children" (2:7, 11). They are loved by God (1:4) and by Paul, who "crooned" (my trans.) over them (2:8). They are called "brethren" eighteen times in this short letter, a number exceeded only by 1 Corinthians, which is more than three times as long.

New relationships came about as a result of conversion and baptism. Paul understood the experience of the Spirit in conversion as a change from ignorance to a knowledge of God. This knowledge was

---

62. Dio Chrysostom *Discourse* 32.11. See above, pp. 3–4, and the literature cited there. See also V. C. Pfitzner, *Paul and the Agon Motif,* NovTSup 16 (Leiden: E. J. Brill, 1967), 28–35, who, however, rejects the interpretation offered here (pp. 112–14).

63. See Rom. 2:9; 2 Cor. 4:8. The combination of joy and affliction also appears in 2 Cor. 2:3–4; 7:4.

expressed in the new self-understanding that the believer was a child of God, but that experience was to Paul possible only in a new community. In his interpretation, the Spirit baptized Jews and Greeks, slave and free, male and female, into one body (cf. 1 Cor. 12:13). The baptismal language in Gal. 3:26—4:6 represents the convert's initiation into the Christian community as an adoption by God through which the convert is admitted into a new family of brothers and sisters. Baptism thus consciously brought about a change in social relationships as well as self-understanding, in both of which members of the Christian community were contrasted with "outsiders."[64]

Members of pagan cults and associations also referred to each other as brothers, but it is generally agreed that the Christian concept of brotherhood developed out of Judaism.[65] Pagans, in fact, took offense at the intimacy that Christians expressed with such language, and scorned it.[66] Being a member of the Christian family carried with it moral responsibilities that distinguished Christians from pagans.[67] Paul had taught his new converts about "love of the brethren," and it is significant that when he reminds them of it, he also stresses their social responsibility and urges positive relationships with the "outsiders" (4:9–12).[68] Like the other converts we have seen, the Thessalonians too were redefining their relationship with the larger society.

The desire to reinforce his readers' sense of community may partially explain Paul's use of kinship language in 1 Thessalonians, but there must have been other reasons for his concerted use of family terms. His heavy use of such language in 1 Corinthians can partly be explained by the divisions in Corinth that he wanted to heal, but there is no evidence that the Thessalonians were similarly divided.

64. On the baptismal language, see W. A. Meeks, "The Image of the Androgyne: Some Uses of a Symbol in Earliest Christianity," *HR* 13 (1974): 165–208, and on the use of kinship language, Meeks, *First Urban Christians,* 86–89. Cf. H. D. Betz, "Spirit, Freedom, and Law: Paul's Message to the Galatian Churches," *SEA* 39 (1974): 151–52.

65. See Meeks, *First Urban Christians,* 87; cf. K. H. Schelkle, "Bruder," *RAC* 2 (1954): 632–39; B. Kötting, "Genossenschaft," *RAC* 10 (1978): 144–45.

66. E.g., Lucian *Peregrinus* 13, and the pagan views reflected in Minucius Felix *Octavius* 9.2; 31.8; Tertullian *Apology* 39. See further Malherbe, *Social Aspects,* 40 n. 26.

67. Cf. 1 Cor. 5:11–13; 6:1–6. Christians have a special responsibility to one another: Gal. 6:10.

68. See pp. 95–107 for a more extensive discussion of this passage.

It is possible to detect in this use another problem caused by missionary movements, namely, the dividing of households. Philosophers had to come to terms with the problem, and so did Christians, who were regarded as domestic troublemakers.[69] Entire households did not always convert, and the strains in relationship that resulted posed major problems. The Synoptic Gospel tradition, especially, reflects the domestic division that Christianity caused:

> Do you think that I have come to give peace on earth? No, I tell you, but rather division; for henceforth in one house there will be five divided, three against two and two against three; they will be divided, father against son and son against father, mother against daughter and daughter against her mother, mother-in-law against her daughter-in-law and daughter-in-law against her mother-in-law.[70]
>
> (Luke 12:51–53)

It also, however, promised a substitute.

> Truly, I say to you, there is no one who has left house or brothers or sisters or mother or father or children or lands, for my sake and for the gospel, who will not receive a hundredfold now in this time, houses and brothers and sisters and mothers and children and lands, with persecutions, and in the age to come eternal life.
>
> (Mark 10:29–30)

The new relationships in a house church like Jason's helped to compensate for the broken natural relationships,[71] and this may very well be the reason for Paul's emphasis.

There may also be a more specific reason for Paul's concentrated use of kinship language. In other New Testament writings in which there is evidence of domestic tensions, whether caused by mixed marriage (1 Corinthians 7; 1 Peter 3:1–6) or relations with slaves (Philemon), the language of kinship is also concentrated. Such language appears to compensate for the natural relationships which were broken or placed under stress, or else is exploited to describe the

---

69. See the collection of material in A. von Harnack, *Mission and Expansion* (chap. 1, n. 3), 1:393–98; cf. Dodds, *Pagan and Christian* (n. 4 above), 115–16.

70. Cf. Matt. 10:21, 34–38; Mark 13:12; Luke 21:16. See D. L. Balch, *Let Wives Be Submissive: The Domestic Code in 1 Peter*, SBLMS 26 (Chico, Calif.: Scholars Press, 1981).

71. See Klauck, *Hausgemeinde und Hauskirche* (chap. 1, n. 31), 56–60.

new relationships within the community.[72] In 1 Thess. 4:3–8 and 1 Corinthians 7, Paul gives advice on marriage, the only two instances of such advice in his letters. The exegetical difficulties abound, but Paul's points of concern are clear. That marriage needs to be discussed here in 1 Thessalonians is an important indication of the social redefinition that the recent converts had to undergo.

Paul's stress on the motivations for the conduct he advises may be new, but instruction in marriage was not. His instruction had already been received by his converts during the period when he was shaping the community (1 Thess. 4:1–2, 6). His instruction in 1 Thessalonians is thus a continuation of his advice to members of the new, Christian community. That marriage is to be entered "in holiness and honor, not in the passion of lust like heathen who do not know God" (4:4–5), betrays the sharpness of the community's redefinition with respect to non-Christians. And Paul's direction that, in marrying, the Christian should not "transgress, and wrong his brother in this matter" (4:6), whatever it may mean in detail, points to the communal dimension of marriage within the group.[73]

The Thessalonians, then, appear to have shared much with the other converts we have described earlier. Their conversion resulted in distress and dejection which threatened their adherence to the faith. Their feeling of isolation, heightened by opposition or suspicion from non-Christians, was exacerbated by Paul's abrupt departure. When he says that he prays that he might see them face-to-face and supply what is lacking in their faith (3:10), he reflects their sense of inadequacy, a self-estimation resembling the dissatisfaction of Plutarch's disciples with the slowness of their progress. The Thessalonians' social relationships within the community, as well as between the community and the wider society, were being redefined, evidently not without stress. These conditions had intensified by the time Paul wrote to them. In 1 Thess. 5:14–15, he names three classes of people in need of exhortation: the disorderly (probably persons

72. E.g., 1 Cor. 7:12–15; Philemon 7, 10, 16, 20; 1 Pet. 2:17; 5:9.
73. See Malherbe, "Exhortation in First Thessalonians," *NovT* 25 (1983): 250–51; O. L. Yarbrough, *"Not Like the Gentiles": Marriage Rules in the Letters of Paul*, SBLDS 80 (Atlanta: Scholars Press, 1985), 65–87.

who did not conform to the standards or requirements of the community), the discouraged, and the weak. In addition, his readers were sorrowing because of the death of some members of the community (4:13). Except for the latter, it is likely that all these conditions already existed to some degree during Paul's sojourn with them and that he had to take them into consideration as he shaped the individuals into a community.

## PAUL AS PARADIGM FOR THE COMMUNITY

In attempting to discover how Paul shaped the Thessalonians into a community we must begin with his claim, "And you became imitators of us and of the Lord" (1 Thess. 1:6). Paul usually calls his readers to imitation.[74] This description of the Thessalonian church's origin, however, is the only place where Paul refers to converts who had already modeled themselves after him. In short, Paul's method of shaping a community was to gather converts around himself and by his own behavior to demonstrate what he taught. In doing this, he followed a widely practiced method of his day, particularly by moral philosophers.[75]

It is natural that converts would look for guidance to the person who had brought them to conversion, and we have seen that Musonius Rufus consciously offered his own conduct as an example to his disciples.[76] Seneca further illustrates the importance that was attached to the personal example of a mentor. Seneca promises his correspondent that he would send him books of instruction, but then continues:

> Of course, however, the living voice and the intimacy of a common life will help you more than the written word. You must go to the scene of the action, first, because men put more faith in their eyes than in their ears, and second, because the way is long if one follows precepts, but short and helpful, if one follows patterns. Cleanthes could not have been the express image of Zeno, if he had merely heard his lectures; he shared in his life, saw into his hidden purposes, and

74. See 1 Cor. 4:16; 11:1; Phil. 3:17; cf. 2 Thess. 3:7, 9.
75. On the use of personal examples, see B. Fiore, *The Function of Personal Example in the Socratic and Pastoral Epistles,* AnBib 105 (Rome: Biblical Institute, 1986). For the importance of personal examples in psychagogy, see esp. Hadot, *Seneca* (chap. 1, n. 60), 164–65.
76. See p. 20.

watched him to see whether he lived according to his own rules. Plato, Aristotle, and the whole throng of sages who were destined to go each his different way, derived more benefit from the character than from the words of Socrates. It was not the class-room of Epicurus, but living together under the same roof, that made great men out of Metrodorus, Hermarchus, and Polyaenus. Therefore I summon you, not merely that you may derive benefit, but that you may confer benefit; for we can assist each other greatly.

(Seneca *Epistle* 6.5–6)

The pattern provided by a teacher's life was prized because it lent concreteness to his teaching, thereby making it more persuasive.

The teacher as model provided more than a moral paradigm. The teacher also offered security to those who looked to him for guidance. Seneca therefore advises his reader:

"Cherish some man of high character, and keep him ever before your eyes, living as if he were watching you, and ordering all your actions as if he beheld them." Such, my dear Lucilius, is the counsel of Epicurus; he has quite properly given us a guardian and attendant. We can get rid of most sins, if we have a witness who stands near us when we are likely to go wrong. The soul should have someone to respect,—one by whose authority it may make even its inner shrine more hallowed. Happy is the man who can make others better, not merely when he is in their company, but even when he is in their thoughts! One who can so revere another, will soon be himself worthy of reverence. Choose therefore a Cato; or, if Cato seems too severe a model, choose some Laelius, a gentler spirit. Choose a master whose life, conversation, and soul-expressing face have satisfied you; picture him always to yourself as your protector and your pattern. For we must indeed have someone according to whom we may regulate our characters.[77]

(Seneca *Epistle* 11.8–10)

In the process of exemplifying moral virtue to his disciples, the teacher's relationship with them made possible their continuing security and cultivation of the virtuous life.

Paul's practice in Thessalonica fits this convention of a philosopher offering himself as a paradigm for his followers. Like some philosophers, Paul by his own example had shown his converts that

77. Cf. Seneca *Epistles* 25.5–6; 32.1; 52.8–10; 94.55–59. For the successful imitator in turn becoming an example, cf. Seneca *Epistle* 98. 12–14; Isocrates *Evagoras* 78.

they should earn their own living.[78] And, as we shall see in chapter 3, when in 1 Thessalonians Paul reminds his readers of his example, he does so with a practical, hortatory purpose in mind. But, while he was shaping the community in Thessalonica, the theme of imitation had considerably more than an ethical dimension.

The moral instruction Paul gave his converts took place within a special relationship that Paul as their model fostered. Paul draws attention to this relationship in a number of ways. In writing of the Thessalonians' conversion, he stresses his personal relationship with the unsettled converts by heaping up personal pronouns:

> For we know, brethren beloved by God, that he has chosen *you*; for *our* gospel came to *you* not only in word, but also in power and in the Holy Spirit and with full conviction. You know what kind of men *we* proved to be among *you* for *your* sake. And *you* became imitators of *us* and of the Lord, for *you* received the word in much affliction, with joy inspired by the Holy Spirit; so that *you* became an example.
>
> (1 Thess. 1:4–7, cf. 9)

As with serious philosophers, Paul's life could not be distinguished from what he preached: his life verified his gospel.[79] He struggled as he gave himself to the preaching of the gospel for the benefit of others. So by imitating him the Thessalonians joined him in that giving of self for others.[80] When Paul says that the result of their imitation of him and the Lord was that they in turn had become an example to all the believers in Macedonia and Achaia because they had spread the word of the Lord and their faith had become widely known (1:7–8), he is complimenting them on the success with which they had imitated him. They had met the standards of moral philosophers like Seneca for the ideal relationship between a model and his emulators.

Paul elaborates on this relationship with his converts in 1 Thess. 2:1–12. Here he reminds them of his pastoral care for them while shaping the community. In the description of his activity he

78. 1 Thess. 2:9; cf. 2 Thess. 3:7, 9. See p. 99.

79. See Rigaux, *Aux Thessaloniciens* (n. 60 above), 61–62; Laub, "Paulus als Gemeindegründer" (Introd., n. 2), 26–31.

80. See H. Koester, "Apostel und Gemeinde in den Briefen an die Thessalonicher," in *Kirche. Festschrift für Günther Bornkamm zum 75. Geburtstag*, ed. D. Lührmann and G. Strecker (Tübingen: J. C. B. Mohr [Paul Siebeck], 1980), 288–90.

consciously makes use of descriptions of the ideal moral philosopher. Like the philosophers, Paul had been bold in his speech (*eparrēsiasametha . . . laleisai*, 2:1–2), and his frankness was exercised within a caring relationship.[81] The images that he uses to describe himself further convey the security he attempted to give them.

Paul projects and communicates a pastoral concern particularly appropriate to recent converts who were experiencing distress. He had chosen to be a Laelius rather than a Cato. Although he could have been harsh in making apostolic demands of the Thessalonians while he was with them, he was instead gentle as a wet nurse crooning to her own children (2:6–8). This image was current in Paul's day. It was used to describe the discrimination with which the perceptive philosopher exercised frankness. Plutarch, for example, warns against being frank with someone in difficult circumstances:

> Under such conditions, then, the very circumstances in which the unfortunate find themselves leave no room for frank speaking and sententious saws, but they do require gentle usage and help. When children fall down, the nurses do not rush up to them to berate them, but they take them up, wash them, and straighten their clothes, and, after all this is done, they then rebuke and punish them.[82]
>
> (Plutarch *How to Tell a Flatterer from a Friend* 69BC)

Paul intensifies the image by likening his demeanor to that of a nurse suckling her own children, not merely those under her charge. Paul's reason for such gentleness was that the Thessalonians had become very dear to him, and hence he was prepared to give himself to them.

The same note of concern for their well-being is struck in the claim that he supported himself in order not to burden them (2:9). Although artisans like Paul could be self-sufficient, they suffered deprivation, poverty, and the contempt of those better situated. Paul's decision to engage in manual labor was a sacrifice, for he did not belong to the working class. The reference to his work in this context therefore reveals another understanding of his manual labor: it

81. See pp. 29–33. For the importance of *philia* in the proper exercise of *parrēsia*, see Plutarch *How to Tell a Flatterer from a Friend*. For friendship as the proper relationship within which psychagogy can take place, see Hadot, *Seneca* (chap. 1, n. 60), 164–76. See also n. 95 below.

82. For a more detailed treatment, see Malherbe, "'Gentle as a Nurse': The Cynic Background to I Thess ii," *NovT* 12 (1970), esp. 211–14.

demonstrated how Paul was prepared to give up his social status in order to identify with manual laborers.[83]

Paul also uses the image of a father's concern for his children to describe his pastoral care for the Thessalonians:

> For you know how, like a father with his children, we exhorted (*parakalō*) each one of you and encouraged (*paramytheomai*) you and charged (*martyromai*) you to lead a life worthy of God, who calls you into his own kingdom and glory.
>
> (1 Thess. 2:11–12)

It was common at the time for a moral teacher to exhort his students as their father and to think of them as his children.[84] The teacher's relationship with his hearers transcended natural family relationships. In attempting to benefit his disciples, the philosopher would adapt his words to their needs without sacrificing his integrity, as Dio Chrysostom emphasizes:

> But as for himself, the man of whom I speak will strive to preserve his individuality in seemly fashion and with steadfastness, never deserting his post of duty, but always honouring and promoting virtue and sobriety and trying to lead all men thereto, partly by persuading and exhorting, partly by abusing and reproaching, in the hope that he may thereby rescue somebody from folly and low desires and intemperance and soft living, taking them aside privately one by one and also admonishing them in groups every time he finds the opportunity, with gentle words at times, at others harsh.
>
> (Dio Chrysostom *Discourse* 77/78.38)

Rather than seek his own advantage, the good philosopher would help his friends by cautioning some, consoling others, reconciling brothers, and making peace between husbands and wives.[85] The philosophers therefore recognized the desirability of personalized instruction which could be adapted to the circumstances and needs

---

83. On the circumstances under which Paul worked, see Hock, *Social Context* (chap. 1, n. 40), here esp. 35. On Paul's social status, see Malherbe, *Social Aspects* (chap. 1, n. 5), 29–59. Paul's attitude toward his labor is reflected by the fact that he lists it in a series of hardships (1 Cor. 4:12) and that he regards it as servile (1 Cor. 9:19) and an act of abasement (2 Cor. 11:7).

84. See Malherbe, "Exhortation in First Thessalonians," *NovT* 25 (1983): 243–45.

85. Lucian *Demonax* 8–9.

of individuals.[86] Paul reminds his readers that he too had paid attention to each one of them and that he had adopted different modes of persuasion: exhortation, consolation (RSV: "encouragement"), and insistence (RSV: "charge").

Paul's consolation of his distressed converts must have been a major part of his pastoral care. He reminds them of his instruction:

> You yourselves know that this is to be our lot. For when we were with you, we told you beforehand that we were to suffer affliction; just as it has come to pass, and as you know.[87]
>
> (1 Thess. 3:3-4)

This is similar to the warning given to proselytes in the rite by which they were admitted to the Jewish community.[88] But the method of anticipating hardships also had a counterpart among the moral philosophers of the day,[89] as Seneca illustrates:

> What, have you only at this moment learned that death is hanging over your head, at this moment exile, at this moment grief? You were born to these perils. Let us think of everything that can happen as something which will happen.
>
> (Seneca *Epistle* 24.15)

> Therefore, nothing ought to be unexpected by us. Our minds should be sent forward in advance to meet all problems, and we should consider, not what is wont to happen, but what can happen. For what is there in existence that Fortune, when she has so willed, does not drag down from the very height of its prosperity?
>
> (Seneca *Epistle* 91.4)

Seneca uses two arguments from the long tradition of consolation: Since hardships in all forms befall us because fate so decrees, we

---

86. Cf. Plutarch *On Listening to Lectures* 43E–44A; *How to Tell a Flatterer from a Friend* 70D–71D; Apollonius of Tyana *Epistle* 10; Philo *On the Decalogue* 36–39. See further, Rabbow, *Seelenführung* (n. 6 above), 272–79; Hadot, *Seneca* (chap. 1, n. 60), 64–66; A. J. Malherbe, "'In Season and Out of Season': 2 Timothy 4:2," *JBL* 103 (1984): 235–43.

87. The imperfect tense of *proelegomen* (RSV: "we told you beforehand") indicates that Paul repeatedly instructed on that subject.

88. See p. 44, and cf. W. A. Meeks, "Social Functions of Apocalyptic Language in Pauline Christianity," in *Apocalypticism in the Mediterranean World and the Near East*, ed. D. Hellholm (Tübingen: J. C. B. Mohr [Paul Siebeck], 1983), 692.

89. Rabbow, *Seelenführung* (n. 6 above), 160–71; Hadot, *Seneca* (chap. 1, n. 60), 59–61. Cf. Epictetus *Discourse* 3.24.103–4 (p. 83 below).

should not be surprised by them, and we can overcome them by anticipating them. John Chrysostom was aware that Paul was referring to this method of consolation.[90]

It should now be evident that Paul's method of pastoral care had distinct similarities to the "pastoral care" of contemporary moral philosophers. The way Paul describes his activity, particularly his use of the images of nurse and father, makes it clear that he consciously availed himself of their tradition of care. There were, however, also distinct differences between Paul and the philosophers, most notably in their understanding of themselves and their tasks but also in the way they carried out their tasks.[91]

Paul speaks with greater confidence about himself as having already been imitated than did most. The philosophers tended to refer in their exhortations to other individuals as exemplifications of certain virtues; Paul, by contrast, offered himself as a model, in association with the Lord. However, Paul's confidence in offering himself as a paradigm for the community did not reside in his own accomplishments. This is clear from the way in which he describes the Thessalonians' conversion:

> our gospel came to you not only in word, but also in power and in the Holy Spirit and with full conviction.
>
> (1 Thess. 1:5)

A philosopher would have said that *he* had come not only in word but also in deed, thus drawing attention to his own accomplishments as warrants for his demands.[92] Paul, by contrast, draws attention to *God's* initiative and power. God chose them (1:4), and what Paul spoke was not a human message (2:14) but the gospel or word of God (2:2, 9, 13) or the Lord (1:8). According to Paul's understanding, therefore, the Thessalonians became imitators of him as divine power, manifested in the gospel, was reflected in his life.

90. John Chrysostom *Homilies on First Thessalonians, Homily* 4 (PG 62:417). For elements of the consolation tradition in 1 Thess. 4:13–18, see Malherbe, "Exhortation in First Thessalonians," *NovT* 25 (1983): 254–56.

91. For a more detailed discussion, see Malherbe, "Exhortation in First Thessalonians," *NovT* 25 (1983): 246–49.

92. On the requirement that one's words should conform to one's deeds, see Seneca *Epistle* 108.35–37; Dio Chrysostom *Discourse* 70.6; Lucian *Peregrinus* 19. For conformity of life and boldness of speech as warrant for offering oneself as an example, see Lucian *Demonax* 3.

Paul, like the philosophers, spoke boldly in the face of hardship and persecution. Unlike their boldness, his was not based on a moral freedom gained by reason and exercise of the will. It was given by God (2:1–5). The reference to his suffering therefore does not magnify his own courage, nor does it justify harshness, as such references did for the philosophers.[93] Instead, Paul uses images that consistently reveal his caring gentleness. These images were derived from the philosophic moralists. What is striking about Paul's use of these images, however, is that they are not balanced by statements about the necessity of abusiveness and scolding, again unlike the philosophers. That Paul's demeanor was characteristically gentle, and that he was not here engaged in special pleading, is seen from his self-defense in 2 Corinthians 10—13.[94]

The philosopher out of goodwill sought to benefit his listeners with exhortation but was governed by a concern that his integrity not be compromised.[95] Paul also begins a self-description by stressing his integrity (2:1–6), but he emphasizes his own self-giving to a degree that the philosophers did not. He had begotten his converts through the gospel (cf. 1 Cor. 4:16); as their father he was prepared to give himself to them. Moreover, unlike the philosophers who aimed at the development of prudence and virtue in their disciples, Paul adapted himself to the needs of his converts, to the end that they "lead a life worthy of God, who calls [them] into his own kingdom and glory" (2:12). This eschatological perspective also makes Paul's consolation of the distressed converts (3:3–4) different from that of Seneca. Unlike Seneca, Paul did not attribute Christian experience to arbitrary fate. Nor did Paul think that victory over life's vicissitudes was purely an attainment of the rational person. Nor did he strive to become impassive, as the Stoics did (cf. 3:7; 2 Cor. 1:3–7). Rather, Christians have confidence in God, who has their salvation in mind and who has a hand in human affairs (cf. 5:9).

93. See Koester, "Apostel und Gemeinde" (n. 80 above), 290–91.
94. See Malherbe, "Antisthenes and Odysseus, and Paul at War," *HTR* 76 (1983): 143–73. The debate reflects the philosophers' discussions about the proper self-understanding of someone who would dare to benefit others.
95. For goodwill as a motivation for frank speech, see Dio Chrysostom *Discourses* 32.7, 11, 96; 38.9; 51.5; Epictetus *Discourse* 3.22.81. For friendship, see Cicero *On Friendship* 89–90; Seneca *Epistle* 29.1–3. See pp. 84–86.

There are, then, considerable differences between Paul and the philosophers, but the methods Paul used were nevertheless derived from the philosophers. We have focused on the way in which Paul formed a community rather than on the teaching which, in Paul's view, was the means by which God created the fellowship. It goes without saying that Paul would have had to engage persistently in the intellectual reconstruction and ethical modification of his converts.[96] Such instruction may have assumed a distinct, even partially fixed, pattern without taking the form of a catechism, as has been argued. Leaving that issue aside, one cannot miss the fact that 1 Thessalonians repeatedly refers to instruction that the readers had received from Paul.[97] Except for references to Paul's mission preaching (1:9–10) and eschatological instruction (4:6; 5:1–2), it is striking that Paul reminds them of things that are not in the first instance doctrinal or theological. The greatest stress is on the relationships that were developed both between the Thessalonians and Paul (2:1, 5, 9, 10) and among themselves (4:9–10), on sexual morality (4:3–8), and on the distress they would continue to suffer for their faith (3:3–4).

Paul refers to these items because it was appropriate to do so at the time he wrote the letter. It may be questioned whether they figured as prominently at the time of the church's formation as they do in the letter. If it is accepted that Paul wrote only a matter of months after founding this church, and if our interpretation of the Thessalonians' emotional state and social relationships has merit, then it is unlikely that their circumstances would have changed enough to require Paul to change his emphasis.

As Paul's frequent references to what they already knew and were doing indicate, he was concerned to underline the continuity between his association with them in the past and at the time he wrote the letter. What had changed? Paul was no longer with them and they had been plunged into grief by the death of some of their members (4:13). So when Paul wrote to them they had a problem: How was this community that was formed around Paul going to survive under such conditions without their paradigm? Paul had shaped a community. Now he had to provide for its continuing nurture.

96. See Holmberg, *Paul and Power* (Introd., n. 4), 70–74.
97. See pp. 74–76.

# 3

# Nurturing the Community

As an itinerant preacher, Paul could claim that he had preached throughout the eastern Mediterranean (Rom. 15:19). His mobility enabled him to found many churches; it also caused him great anxiety for the conventicles he left behind. Relatively unorganized, fraught with distress, with only rudimentary instruction in the faith, and in tension with the larger society, they were anything but stable when he left them. They furthermore continued to grow and expanded their influence, as is said of the Thessalonians (1 Thess. 1:7–8). Therefore the possibility was good that the communities' conditions would change from what they were when Paul left them. It is no wonder that Paul was preoccupied in his letters with his enforced separation and that he listed, as his chief apostolic hardship, "the daily pressure upon me of my anxiety for all the churches" (2 Cor. 11:28).

Paul continued, even in his absence, to nurture the churches he had founded and shaped. First Thessalonians provides us with an excellent opportunity to observe how he did so. The letter reveals his sensitivity to the psychological and social conditions of his converts, particularly their distress and sense of isolation, their feeling that he had abandoned them after forming the community around himself, and their feeling of inadequacy in their new faith. Paul responds to their needs in three ways: by sending Timothy as his emissary, by writing the letter, and by directing them to continue among themselves the nurture he had begun.

61

## TIMOTHY'S MISSION

Renewed attention has recently been given to the importance of fellow workers in Paul's mission.[1] Although attention is normally focused on Paul, it is clear that his mission was a collective enterprise and that his co-workers performed a wide range of functions. Their roles can be viewed from the perspective of the governance of the church or the distribution of power in the mission, as has most recently been done,[2] but I want to examine more narrowly Timothy's role in Paul's effort to further the religious development of his Thessalonian converts. The Book of Acts pictures Silas as the more prominent of Paul's associates in Thessalonica (Acts 17:4, 10, 14) and always mentions him before Timothy, as Paul also does (1 Thess. 1:1; 2 Cor. 1:19). Despite the prominence of Silas, however, it was Timothy who was Paul's emissary to Thessalonica.

The circumstances responsible for Paul's departure from Thessalonica and the subsequent movements of Silas and Timothy have been debated at great length.[3] Although Acts 17:5–10 ascribes responsibility for Paul's departure to events initiated by the Jews, Paul does not explicitly comment on his reasons for leaving the city. However, if his statement that the Jews "drove us out" (1 Thess. 2:15) refers to Thessalonica, and the passive "we were bereft of you" (2:17) is taken seriously, they do support the view that Paul left Thessalonica involuntarily because of Jewish opposition. According to Acts 17:11–15, after a short stay in Beroea, Paul was again forced to move on, this time to Athens, from where he summoned Silas and Timothy to leave Beroea and join him in Athens. Acts does not record that either of them did, and it is futile to speculate on their movements, particularly those of Silas. According to 1 Thessalonians, Paul was repeatedly frustrated in his attempts to return to Thessalonica (2:17–18), and he therefore sent Timothy from Athens (3:1–2, 5). Why he did not send the more experienced Silas, if Silas had indeed also made it to Athens, we do not know; more significant for the Pauline mission is that this event

1. See p. 14 n. 35. Cf. E. E. Ellis, "Paul and His Co-Workers," *NTS* 17 (1971): 437–52.
2. Meeks, *First Urban Christians*, 55–63; Holmberg, *Paul and Power*, 57–70.
3. For extensive discussion of the issues, see the introduction to my commentary on 1 Thessalonians in the Anchor Bible (forthcoming).

marks the emergence of Timothy as a major figure in the  mission. Thus, after a sojourn of two or three months in Thessalonica, and at most three or four months after leaving the newly formed church, Paul sent Timothy to them.

The circumstances surrounding Timothy's mission and return are described in 1 Thess. 2:17—3:10. Neither here nor elsewhere in the letter does Paul give any indication that he had dispatched Timothy upon receiving disconcerting news—or, for that matter, any news—from or about the Thessalonians. The impression that Paul skillfully creates is that it was as much *his* circumstances as the Thessalonians' need which necessitated Timothy's visit. Yet the passion with which Paul writes this section shows that he was acutely aware of a pressing need to maintain contact with the Thessalonians. Paul frequently expresses his concern about being separated from his churches,[4] but his language in 1 Thessalonians is particularly poignant. The reason is obvious. In no other letter does he write to people who had been Christians for so short a time and who were therefore especially in need of encouragement, preferably through personal contact.

To appreciate Paul's pastoral intention and method, it is necessary to examine his understanding of the purpose of Timothy's mission. We are again, however, faced with the possibility that his account may be shaped more by his strategy at the time he later wrote 1 Thessalonians than that it accurately reflects the original intention of Timothy's mission. Yet the continuing emotional condition of his converts, the sense of continuity one gains from chapters 1—3, and the warmheartedness of the entire letter justify our taking Paul's comments about Timothy's mission at face value.

The passion with which Paul recites the events that had led up to Timothy's return to him is striking. It makes startlingly vivid Paul's statement of his and the Thessalonians' mutual need to maintain contact. Paul begins by describing his own need (2:17-20). He had been made an orphan by a temporary physical, but not spiritual, separation from them. Momentarily changing from the epistolary plural that he had been using thus far in the letter, he refers to himself

4. 1 Cor. 4:18-21; 5:3-4; 16:1-7; 2 Cor. 1:15—2:1; 7:5-7; Phil. 1:27; 2:12.

by name ("I Paul," 2:18) in order to heighten the emotional impact.[5]
He had made extraordinary, repeated attempts to visit them, but
Satan had hindered him. The reasons for his anguished efforts are
contained in a series of exclamations that describe his affection for
the Thessalonians: They are his hope, joy, crown of victory in which
he might boast and glory.[6] For that reason, when he could no longer
endure the separation, he resolved to be abandoned, left alone in
Athens, while Timothy went to establish them in their faith and
exhort them. The events that led to Timothy's mission are therefore
described in terms of *Paul's* circumstances and yearning for them.
He had been orphaned by circumstances beyond his control, but his
sending of Timothy was a voluntary act that left him still more
desolate in Athens. He was prepared to do so because he could not
bear the uncertainty about Satan's effect on their faith and the out-
come of his own work among them (3:1–3).

This description reveals Paul's awareness of a major difficulty
faced by recent converts—the feeling that they had been forsaken,
sometimes expressed by describing themselves as orphans. Paul
forcibly makes the point that the separation is involuntary, but he
does so in a manner that reflects his pastoral sensitivity. His explana-
tion is not merely a justification of himself; rather, it reveals an identification with the Thessalonians in their abandonment. Through
their separation, Paul too had been made an orphan, and he was
willing to suffer further loneliness on their behalf. It has been suggested that Timothy carried a letter from Paul to the Thessalonians
in which Paul already addressed the issue.[7] It is impossible to determine whether Paul did write such a letter, but it can be assumed that

---

5. "I, Paul" is emphatic not only because of *egō* but because Paul uses his own name
in the body of the letter. He seldom refers to himself by name. The self-references in
2 Cor. 10:1 and Philemon 9 appear in appeals (*parakalein*) and heighten the emotion, as
they do in other ancient letters of friendship. See H. Koskenniemi, *Studien zur Idee und
Phraseologie des griechischen Briefes bis 400 n. Chr.*, Annales Academiae Scientarum
Fennicae, Series B, vol. 102.2 (Helsinki: Suomalainen Tiedeakatemia, 1956), 124.
In Koskenniemi's examples, however, the self-references by name are made at the
end of letters.

6. For Paul's churches as the ground of his boasting and their security in the faith
as a standard by which he will be judged, see G. Lyons, *Pauline Autobiography:
Toward a New Understanding,* SBLDS 73 (Atlanta: Scholars Press, 1985), 210–14.

7. J. R. Harris ("A Study in Letter-Writing," *The Expositor,* 5th series, 8 [1898]: 173)
surmised that traces of such a letter are discernible in 1 Thess. 2:17; 3:2, 5, 6.

Timothy orally conveyed Paul's concerns, probably recounting Paul's feeling that he had been orphaned by his separation from them.

Paul provides more information about the reason and significance of Timothy's mission in two statements on its purpose (1 Thess. 3:2–3 and 3:5) and in his description of Timothy's report upon his return (3:6–10). The first purpose ostensibly had the Thessalonians' benefit in view: Timothy was sent to establish them in their faith and exhort them, "that no one be moved (*sainesthai*) by these afflictions (*thlipsesin*)." It is clear that Paul was concerned that they might be unsettled emotionally,[8] but there is little agreement on the nature of the *thlipseis* or indeed whether "these afflictions" were Paul's or the Thessalonians'. Commentators generally think that Paul is referring to the Thessalonians' persecution (2:14). Some, however, have seen here a reference to Paul's experiences just recounted in 2:17–3:2, which would have been unsettling to the Thessalonians. Others think both the Thessalonians' and Paul's afflictions are in view.[9]

The main reason for referring the afflictions to the Thessalonians is that *thlipsis* is thought to denote persecution. We have seen that it does not always do so and that it does not in 1:6, where it describes the distress of new converts. Furthermore, 2:17 begins a new section of the letter, which makes a reference to 2:14 unlikely. In highly affective language Paul has described his sense of deprivation caused by their separation, and it is reasonable to understand "these afflictions" as his distress brought about by the separation, particularly since in 3:7 he explicitly refers to the comfort that Timothy's report brought him in his distress and affliction.[10] As he had identified with the Thessalonians by writing as an orphan, he does by speaking of his own distress.

8. For this meaning of *sainesthai,* see the material collected in von Dobschütz, *Die Thessalonicherbriefe* (chap. 2, n. 60), 133 n. 3; Rigaux, *Aux Thessaloniciens* (chap. 2, n. 60), 470–71; cf. H. Chadwick, "I Thess. 3.3, *sainesthai,*" *JTS* N.S. 1 (1950): 156–58.

9. The Thessalonians: Frame, *The Epistles of St. Paul* (chap. 2, n. 56), 127; Rigaux, *Aux Thessaloniciens* (chap. 2, n. 60), 472; Bruce, *1 & 2 Thessalonians* (chap. 2, n. 56), 62. Paul: John Chrysostom *Homilies on First Thessalonians,* Homily 3 (PG 62: 442); von Dobschütz, *Thessalonicherbriefe,* 134–35. The Thessalonians and Paul: Best, *Commentary* (chap. 2, n. 57), 135.

10. Commentators are divided on whether the distress and tribulation were external or internal, with the majority favoring the former. Bruce (*1 & 2 Thessalonians* [chap. 2, n. 56], 67) correctly thinks they may have been more psychological than physical.

Paul thus reminds the Thessalonians that he had sent Timothy because *he* could not endure the separation. By stating his concern that *his* afflictions might discourage and unsettle them to the point of abandoning the faith, Paul was not arrogant but diplomatic and pastorally sensitive. He identifies with their distress, and his assumption that they reciprocate his affection and care for their well-being is an indirect compliment to them which lent strength to the friendly relationship between them, which provides the basis for the advice he would give in 1 Thessalonians.[11] Thus, while the first stated purpose of Timothy's mission was to strengthen the Thessalonians, the mission was an expression of Paul's conviction that their faith was bound to their relationship with him.

The second statement of purpose is more explicit in expressing Paul's personal interest (1 Thess. 3:5). He draws attention to that interest by using the emphatic *kagō* ("and I"), again lapsing into the singular ("I sent"), and by claiming their perseverance in the faith as proof of the success of his labor. The connection between Paul and the Thessalonians is further accentuated by showing them as pitted against the same adversary: as Satan prevented Paul's return to them (2:18), so the tempter might seduce them from the faith (3:5).

Paul's account of Timothy's return and his own reaction to it (1 Thess. 3:6–10) reveals more clearly what he had intended to achieve by sending Timothy. Paul wrote 1 Thessalonians immediately after Timothy's return, and his reaction to the report exudes relief and joy because their faith was intact (3:6–8), even though it needed to be supplemented (3:10). What receives more comment, however, is what Timothy had to report about the Thessalonians' attitude toward Paul. Timothy brought back the good news (*euangelisamenou*) about their faith and love, and that they continued to hold Paul in good remembrance and yearned to see him.[12] In response, Paul twice assures them that he yearns to see them, tells them how he was comforted by Timothy's news, and thanks God for the joy which he feels for their sake.

11. This interpretation rules out the possibility that there was any tension between Paul and the Thessalonians. For the emphasis on reciprocity between them, see Lyons, *Pauline Autobiography* (n. 6 above), 216.

12. Whether the Thessalonians expressed their attitude toward Paul in a letter that also contained requests for direction on matters that troubled them need not concern us. See the discussion in my Anchor Bible commentary (forthcoming).

The Thessalonians already knew the other autobiographical details to which Paul refers. It is significant that his new information deals with their attitude toward him. They continued to love him and hold him in good remembrance.[13] The latter does not simply mean that they remembered him kindly (RSV), thought kindly of him (NEB), or had pleasant memories of him (NIV). Rather, the statement is to be understood in the light of the practice, followed by Paul, of offering oneself as an example who would lend security to one's students and make possible their moral and spiritual development. When one was separated from one's teacher, one yearned for him and remembered in detail what he taught and the example he set. Lucian illustrates the attitude of the new convert toward his absent teacher:

> Then, too, I take pleasure in calling his words to mind frequently, and have already made it a regular exercise: even if nobody happens to be at hand, I repeat them to myself two or three times a day just the same. I am in the same case with lovers. In the absence of the objects of their fancy they think over their actions and their words, and by dallying with these beguile their lovesickness into the belief that they have their sweethearts near; in fact, sometimes they even imagine they are chatting with them and are as pleased with what they formerly heard as if it were just being said, and by applying their minds to the memory of the past give themselves no time to be annoyed by the present. So I too, in the absence of my mistress Philosophy, get no little comfort out of gathering together the words that I then heard and turning them over to myself. In short, I fix my gaze on that man as if he were a lighthouse and I were adrift at sea in the dead of night, fancying him by me whenever I do anything and always hearing him repeat his former words. Sometimes, especially when I put pressure on my soul, his face appears to me and the sound of his voice abides in my ears. Truly, as the comedian says, "he left a sting implanted in his hearers!"[14]

(Lucian *Nigrinus* 6–7)

In Paul's language, the convert continued to love his teacher, yearn for him, and hold him in good remembrance.

---

13. Paul thinks of their love for him rather than for each other or God. Cf. W. Marxsen, *Der erste Brief an die Thessalonicher,* Zürcher Bibelkommentare (Zürich: Theologischer Verlag, 1979), 55; Lyons, *Pauline Autobiography* (n. 6 above), 55. Best (*Commentary* [chap. 2, n. 57], 140) correctly thinks of their love as manifested in their remembrance of him.

14. Cf. also Seneca, above, p. 53.

Paul's relief and joy, then, were occasioned by the report that the Thessalonians still looked to him as their model. Paul's enforced absence had caused him to worry that they no longer regarded him in this way. But his concern extended beyond his continuing to provide them with a moral paradigm, for Paul did not think that his life could be distinguished from his gospel.[15] Therefore, if the Thessalonians were tempted to forget him, their faith would be in jeopardy. That is why he says that Timothy proclaimed the gospel (*euangelisamenou*) of their faith and love and that they retained a good memory of him.[16]

In sum, Paul's recounting of Timothy's mission and subsequent report reflects Paul's awareness of the Thessalonians' condition as well as his pastoral method. He was conscious of their sense of desolation, which had been aggravated by his absence, was uncertain whether their faith could withstand the emotional stress caused by knowledge of his own experiences, and knew that their faith needed to be supplemented. He sent Timothy as his emissary to establish them further in their faith and exhort them. But Paul's major purpose was to ascertain that his converts still felt bound in love to him and that they continued to look to him for guidance in the faith. Assured by Timothy that they did, Paul wrote 1 Thessalonians, in which he sought, as a substitute for personal conversation, to supply what was still lacking in their faith (3:10).

## PAUL'S PASTORAL LETTER

Paul wrote 1 Thessalonians with a pastoral purpose in mind. By so doing, he created something new.[17] He had pagan predecessors, however, who had also turned to letters as a means by which to shape, instruct, and exhort individuals and communities. Epicurus (342–270 B.C.) did so, and his letters were still well known in Paul's

15. See chap. 2, nn. 79–80.
16. See Best, *Commentary* (chap. 2, n. 57), 139–40; Marxsen, *Der erste Brief* (n. 13 above), 55; Collins, *Studies* (chap. 2, n. 59), 221–22.
17. See esp. H. Koester, "I Thessalonians—Experiment in Christian Writing," in *Continuity and Discontinuity in Church History: Essays Presented to George Huntston Williams on the Occasion of His 65th Birthday*, ed. F. F. Church and T. George (Leiden: E. J. Brill, 1979), 33–44. Koester does not, however, do justice to the epistolographic tradition represented by Epicurus and Seneca. His view of Paul's letters as "instruments of ecclesiastical policy" for use in organizing churches calls to mind Epicurus's letters. Cf. Koester, *Introduction to the New Testament* (chap. 1, n. 18), 2:55, 281, 286.

day, but unfortunately only fragments of some of them have been preserved.[18] Seneca, the Roman Stoic who was a contemporary of Paul, carried on the tradition in an extensive correspondence with his friend Lucilius.[19] As Paul had adopted some of the techniques of the moral philosophers when he founded the church in Thessalonica and adapted them according to his understanding of himself and his task, so did he adapt the convention of writing letters to continue the nurture of his converts. To appreciate Paul's accomplishment in creating a new, Christian, literary product as well as his pastoral method, one ought to be aware of certain features of letter writing at the time.

Letter writing was well established in the first century, and it was self-consciously discussed by rhetorical theorists and writers of letters themselves.[20] A letter was frequently defined as one half of a dialogue. A substitute for one's presence, a letter was expected to contain what one would have said had one been present and to say it in a style appropriate to the occasion. Handbooks on letter writing contained extensive discussions and classifications of these letter styles, one of which, that of the friendly letter (*philikos typos*), is of special interest to us.

It was widely assumed that a major function of a letter was to maintain friendship. Friendship also provided the context for moral instruction.[21] A letter overcame the distance between friends by allowing them to converse with each other and to exhort, entreat, advise, and correct.[22] Friends counted on such guidance from persons

18. The fragments are conveniently collected in the edition of G. Arrighetti, *Epicuro. Opere: Introduzione, testo critico, traduzione e note,* 2d ed. (Florence: Einaudi, 1973). On Epicurus's pastoral letters as precursors of Paul's letters, see Schmid, "Epikur," *RAC* 5 (1962): 743; P. Vielhauer, *Geschichte der urchristlichen Literatur* (Berlin: Walter de Gruyter, 1975), 61–62; H. D. Betz, *2 Corinthians 8 and 9,* Hermeneia (Philadelphia: Fortress Press, 1985), 131. The fragmentary character of the remains has thus far inhibited research that might cast new light on Paul's letters.

19. See esp. Hadot, *Seneca* (chap. 1, n. 60).

20. See A. J. Malherbe, "Ancient Epistolary Theorists," *Ohio Journal of Religious Studies* 5 (1977): 3–77, for what follows. A new edition is to appear in SBLSBS.

21. On the friendly or philophronetic aspect of letters, see A. M. Guillemin, *Pline et la vie littéraire de son temps* (Paris: Les Belles Lettres, 1929), 3ff.; Koskenniemi, *Studien* (n. 5 above), 35–37; Hadot, *Seneca* (chap. 1, n. 60), 65–70.

22. See Cicero *On Friendship* 44 and *Letters to His Friends* 5.17.3; Seneca *Epistles* 16.1–2; 27.1; 40.1; 75.1.

who had more experience,[23] and in their own letters revealed themselves to their friends.[24] The cordiality of such letters of friendship is exemplified by a sample letter provided by one of the handbooks:

> Even though I have been separated from you for a long time, I suffer this in body only. For I can never forget you or the impeccable way we were raised together from childhood up. Knowing that I myself am genuinely concerned about your affairs, and that I have worked unstintingly for what is most advantageous to you, I have assumed that you, too, have the same opinion of me and will refuse me in nothing. You will do well, therefore, to give close attention to the members of my household lest they need anything, to assist them in whatever they might need, and to write to us about whatever you should choose.
>
> (Pseudo-Demetrius *Epistolary Types* 1)

Friendly letters sought to keep alive the memories shared by the correspondents; hence they drew attention to experiences shared in the past.[25]

Friendship was more particularly expressed in parenesis, a type of exhortation in which one sought to influence someone's conduct (*paraineō*) rather than to teach something new.[26] Parenesis was used in many types of communication, including letters, and developed certain characteristics.

Parenesis professed to contain nothing new or original. Isocrates, for example, cautions Nicocles: "Do not be surprised that in what I have said there are many things which you know as well as I." Dio Chrysostom admitted that his advice had been given many times before by others.[27] The intention was to give self-evidently good advice, which meant that it was traditional and generally applicable, although the thoughtful teacher adapted it to particular circumstances.[28] To the objection that it was superfluous to give precepts to people who already knew them, it was replied that exhortation is not

---

23. See Cicero *On Duties* 1.147; Pliny *Epistles* 1.14.3–4; 1.12.11–12; 4.17.4–9.

24. See Seneca *Epistles* 40.1; 88.1. Cf. K. Thraede, *Grundzüge griechisch-römische Brieftopik*, Zetemata 48 (Munich: Beck, 1970), 157–61.

25. See Koskenniemi, *Studien* (n. 5 above), 123–27.

26. The discussion of parenesis that follows is based on my treatment of 1 Thessalonians as a parenetic letter in "Hellenistic Moralists and the New Testament," in *ANRW* 2.26 (forthcoming).

27. Isocrates *Nicocles* 40; Dio Chrysostom *Discourse* 17.1–2.

28. Cf. Seneca *Epistles* 94.35; 64.7–10.

teaching but merely engages the attention and arouses us, concentrates the memory, and keeps it from losing its grip.[29] To jog the memory, a writer or speaker might draw attention to the points he makes by repeatedly saying "you know" (*oidate*), or, if the relationship with his audience was cordial, he might claim that it was unnecessary to speak on the subject.[30]

Another important characteristic of parenesis was the use of personal examples. Isocrates provides an illuminating discussion:

> Nay, if you will but recall also your father's principles, you will have from your own house a noble illustration of what I am telling you. For he did *not* belittle virtue *nor* pass his life in indolence; *on the contrary*, he trained his body by toil, and by his spirit he withstood dangers. *Nor* did he love wealth inordinately; *but*, although he enjoyed the good things at his hand as became a mortal, yet he cared for his possessions as if he had been immortal. *Neither* did he order his existence sordidly, *but* was a lover of beauty, munificent in his manner of life, and generous to his friends; and he prized more those who were devoted to him than those who were his kin by blood; for he considered that in the matter of companionship nature is a much better guide than convention, character than kinship, and freedom of choice than compulsion. But all time would fail us if we should try to recount all his activities. On another occasion I shall set them forth in detail; for the present, however, I have produced a sample of the nature of Hipponicus, after whom you should pattern your life as an ensample, regarding this conduct as your law, and striving to imitate and emulate your father's virtue.
>
> (Isocrates *To Demonicus* 9–11)

This passage illustrates numerous features of parenesis: the need to imitate a model, the importance of reminders, and the delineation of the model in antithetic form ("not . . . but") for the sake of emphasis.

Parenetic letters exhibit the same characteristics and are of special interest for the study of 1 Thessalonians. They also refer to worthy examples, which they describe in antitheses,[31] but a writer like Seneca might also explicitly or implicitly refer to himself when exhorting

---

29. Seneca *Epistle* 94.11, 21, 25; cf. 11.9. See also Dio Chrysostom *Discourse* 17.2; Isocrates *Nicocles or the Cyprians* 12.
30. Seneca *Epistle* 94.26; Isocrates *Philip* 105.
31. Seneca *Epistle* 52.8.

others.[32] When a writer offered himself as an example, he thereby committed himself to continue living in the desired manner. Pliny explains: "I mention this, not only to enforce my advice by example, but also that this letter may be a sort of pledge binding me to persevere in the same abstinence in the future."[33] Parenetic letters further betray an awareness that their advice was not new, and that reminder sufficed.[34] The writer further assumes that his readers are already doing what they should; he therefore really need not write,[35] but only encourages them to continue in their actions.[36]

Recent study of Paul's letters has made it increasingly clear that he was familiar with the epistolographic theory and practice of his day.[37] Evidence for his familiarity abounds in 1 Thessalonians, especially in 2:17—3:10; it is bracketed by statements lamenting his absence but assuring his readers of his desire to see them face-to-face. The theme of bodily absence but spiritual presence is a standard feature of epistolographic theory, especially that about letters of friendship,[38] as also the statement that the writer yearns to see his correspondents (3:6).[39] The writer sometimes accentuates his loneliness by describing himself as an orphan, as Paul does (2:17; cf. 3:1).[40] Paul's reference to himself as an orphan therefore serves the epistolographic function of stressing his desire for communication

32. H. Cancik, *Untersuchungen zu Senecas epistulae morales*, Spudasmata 18 (Hildesheim: Georg Olms, 1967), 68–113.

33. Pliny *Epistle* 7.1.7.

34. Seneca *Epistle* 13.15; Pliny *Epistle* 8.24.1.

35. Cicero *To His Friends* 1.4.3; 2.4.2 and *To His Brother Quintus* 1.1.18, 36.

36. Cicero *To His Friends* 6.10b.4 and *To His Brother Quintus* 1.1.8; Seneca *Epistles* 1.1; 5.1; 13.15; 24.16; 25.4; Ignatius *Polycarp* 1.2; *Ephesians* 4.1; 8.1; *Romans* 2.1; *Trallians* 2.2.

37. On 1 Corinthians, see M. Bünker, *Briefformular und rhetorische Disposition im 1. Korintherbrief*, GTA 28 (Göttingen: Vandenhoeck & Ruprecht, 1984); on 2 Corinthians, see H. Windisch, *Der zweite Korintherbrief*, KEK (Göttingen: Vandenhoeck & Ruprecht, 1924), 75, 82, 84, 211, 414, and now Betz, *2 Corinthians 8 and 9* (n. 18 above), 129–40; on Galatians, Betz, *Galatians*, Hermeneia (Philadelphia: Fortress Press, 1979), 14–15, 223, 232–33, etc.

38. See the sample letter of pseudo-Demetrius (p. 70), and cf. 1 Cor. 5:3; 2 Cor. 10:10–11; Phil. 2:12; G. Karlsson, "Formelhaftes in Paulusbriefen?" *Eranos* 54 (1956): 138–41; K. Thraede, "Untersuchungen zum Ursprung und zur Geschichte der christlichen Poesie, II," *JAC* 5 (1963): 141–45; idem, *Grundzüge* (n. 24 above), 95–102; Koskenniemi, *Studien* (n. 5 above), 169–72, 175–80.

39. Thraede, *Grundzüge* (n. 24 above), 165–73.

40. See the papyrus letters, PSI 116, 11–19 and BGU 385, 4–6; cf. Koskenniemi, *Studien* (n. 5 above), 110.

with his correspondents in addition to alluding to their sense of isolation with which he identifies. It was also standard to rejoice and thank the gods when communication had been established (3:9)[41] and assurance given that the writer had not been forgotten (3:6).[42] A further letter would then substitute for the writer's presence and supply the recipient's need (3:10), somewhat in the way Basil begins a letter to a certain widow:

> Judging it to be quite proper for me, both because of my elderly age and because of the sincerity of my spiritual affection, to visit your incomparable Nobility not only in bodily presence, but also when you are absent not to fail you, but by letter to supply the want, now that I have found this fitting messenger for my letter.
>
> (Basil *Epistle* 297)

More such epistolographic features can be enumerated to demonstrate Paul's familiarity with the theory and practice of letter writing, but these suffice for our immediate purpose.[43] They show that in his earliest extant letter Paul consciously used the literary conventions of his day to communicate his anxiety about the Thessalonians and to guide their continuing religious and moral development.

The style in which Paul writes his friendly letter is that of parenesis, which assumed a friendly relationship. The Paul who writes this letter is not an apostle who makes demands of his converts (2:6), but a nursing mother (2:7), father (2:11), and orphan (2:17), who always has the well-being of the Thessalonians at heart. In addition to these images, which describe his relationship to them rather than to God, the texture of his language further strengthens his bond with them.

In view of our analysis of the Thessalonians' condition Paul had in mind, note how affective his language is when he writes to his converts who were distressed, especially in chapters 1—3, where the following are piled on top of each other: thanksgiving (1:2; 2:13; 3:9); faith, hope, and love (1:3); power, Holy Spirit, and full conviction (1:5); distress and affliction (1:6; 3:3–4, 7); suffering and shameful treatment (2:1–2, 14); gentleness, self-giving, and affection (2:7–8; cf. 1:4);

---

41. Koskenniemi, *Studien*, 75–77.
42. Koskenniemi, *Studien*, 123–27.
43. The evidence is discussed in detail in my forthcoming Anchor Bible commentary.

working night and day in order not to be a burden (2:9); endurance (3:1, 5); danger of being shaken in faith (3:3); good news (3:6); yearning to see one another (2:17; 3:6); abandonment and loneliness (3:1); comfort (2:11–12; 3:7); joy (1:6; 2:19–20; 3:9); the pathos of the entire section (2:17—3:10); and the language of kinship. All of the above, with the exception of "brother," is concentrated in the first three chapters. These chapters are autobiographical in the sense that they describe Paul's relationship with the Thessalonians, and his emotive description of that relationship establishes the manner in which he wishes the relationship to be understood—as one formed by shared experiences that had inextricably linked their lives.

It is only in the second part of the letter that Paul gives advice on matters of conduct, but his self-description in chapters 1—3 already serves a hortatory function by reminding them of his example. Paul brackets this autobiographical section with thankgivings that affirm his close relationship with his readers (1:3–7; 3:6–10) which has not been shattered by their separation. The purpose of this section is to strengthen the bond between them and thus prepare for the advice he will give them in chapters 4 and 5. There is no evidence in the letter to suggest that Paul's rehearsal of his dealings with the Thessalonians is a defense against charges that had been brought against him or that he suspected might be leveled at him.[44] Timothy had reported that the Thessalonians did at all times have a good remembrance of Paul, that they still looked to him as their model. Building on that confidence, Paul here delineates the model he considers appropriate to his present purpose by reminding them of the kind of person they had imitated when he had founded the church. His self-description is therefore not apologetic, but parenetic. It is finely tailored to meet the needs of his readers. He explicitly calls to their remembrance his manual labor (2:9), and he implicitly does so by describing his earlier ministry to

---

44. For summaries of the various attempts to discover opponents whom Paul is said to counter in 1 Thessalonians, see Rigaux, *Aux Thessaloniciens* (chap. 2, n. 60), 58–61; Best, *Commentary* (chap. 2, n. 57), 15–22; Marshall, *1 and 2 Thessalonians* (chap. 2, n. 58), 16–20. For the view presented here, see Malherbe, "Hellenistic Moralists" (n. 26 above), and for further refinements, see H. Boers, "The Form Critical Study of Paul's Letters: I Thessalonians as a Case Study," *NTS* 22 (1976): 140–58; D. W. Palmer, "Thanksgiving, Self-Defense, and Exhortation in I Thessalonians 1–3," *Colloquium* 14 (1981): 23–31.

them in the antithetic parenetic style (2:1–12) and by repeatedly referring to things they already know (1:5; 2:1–2, 5, 11; 3:3–4).

In addition to the experiences that had bound them together,
Paul in these chapters describes himself in terms of his pastoral
activity. It is, however, only in general terms that he describes the
way in which he preached the message that led to their conversion:
He had been empowered by God to be bold in speech when making his appeal through the gospel (2:2–3). He rather concentrates
on his actions with and for them after their conversion. Then he
had been gentle as a nursing mother, affectionate, and self-giving
(2:6–9). He had also been like a father to his children, had given
them individual attention by adapting his discourse, whether general exhortation, encouragement or consolation, or more definite
instruction, as circumstances required (2:11–12). When Timothy
was his emissary, he too was sent to establish them in their faith
and exhort them (3:2).

The Paul who writes the letter, which is another surrogate for his
presence, is therefore portrayed as their nurse and father who under-
stands and in the deepest sense sympathizes with them; he constantly
has them in his heart and mind. He prays for an opportunity to visit
them and fill up what is lacking in their faith (3:10), but since a visit
proves to be impossible, he writes the letter.

The picture that is sketched of the Thessalonians in these chapters
is designed to build their confidence. As new converts, they were
experiencing anguish, sorrow, and a sense of isolation. Their faith,
having been strengthened by Timothy, was still in need of being
supplemented. Paul's pastoral concern is evident in what he says
about them. It is God's power that in the first instance brought them
to faith (1:5) and continues to be at work in them (2:13–14). Their
successful imitation of Paul (and the Lord!) led them to become
examples to others in Macedonia and even Achaia, ones who had
commented on their faith (1:7–9). Furthermore, even their suffering
at the hands of their own countrymen was to be seen as an emulation
of the Christians in Judea (2:14). These geographical references serve
to underscore that, while they might be temporarily deprived of
Paul's presence, they nonetheless are not alone in the world but are
members of a worldwide fellowship in which they enjoy exemplary

standing.[45] The frequent use of the parenetic "as you know" subtly makes the point that, despite their novice status in their new faith, they already share a history in the faith that is documented by their own experience.

The second part of the letter (chapters 4 and 5) contains Paul's advice, ostensibly given "to fill up" the most pressing deficiencies in their faith. Here too the parenetic characteristics are evident. The subject matter appears to have been traditional, probably because of its demonstrated relevance to newly planted churches. This does not, however, mean that Paul was not responding to actual problems in Thessalonica. Moral philosophers too recognized the need to adapt advice that was traditional and general in character to particular circumstances.[46] Of greater interest to us than the content of the advice are the parenetic stylistic devices we have identified and their pastoral application by Paul.

The parenetic references to what they already know continue (4:2; 5:2). They are supplemented by reminders of what Paul had taught them (4:2, 6, 11) and they had readily accepted (4:1). Indeed, they have been taught by God (4:9). It is therefore really not necessary for him to write to them (4:9; 5:1); they are already doing what they should, and he only encourages them to do so more and more (4:1, 10; 5:11).

As Paul articulated his exhortation in the manner of a moral philosopher engaged in parenesis during his sojourn with them, he now does similarly in this pastoral letter.[47] As he (2:3, 12) and Timothy (3:2) had exhorted (*parakaleō*) them, so he continues to do in the letter.[48] He had been insistent in charging them (2:12); now he does so when he instructs them in sexual morality

45. See Meeks, *First Urban Christians* (Intro., n. 4), 307–10.

46. D. G. Bradley ("The *Topos* as Form in the Pauline Paraenesis," *JBL* 72 [1953]: 238–46) argues that the items Paul takes up have only a loose, even arbitrary connection with their context. His treatment of parenesis, however, is inadequate. See n. 26 above, and cf. J. C. Brunt, "More on the *Topos* as a New Testament Form," *JBL* 104 (1985): 495–500.

47. See p. 56. For the varieties of persuasion, see Seneca *Epistle* 94.39, 59: *consolatio, dissuasio, adhortatio, obiurgatio, laudatio, admonitio* (cf. *Epistle* 95.34, 65); Musonius Rufus *Fragment* 49: *hortatur, monet, suadet, obiurgat*.

48. 1 Thess. 4:1, 10, 18; 5:11. On the word *parakaleō*, see O. Schmitz and G. Stählin, "Parakalō, paraklēsis," *TDNT* 5 (1967): 773–99.

(4:6).[49] He had directed them to work with their hands; now he repeats an earlier precept that they continue doing so (4:11).[50] He had comforted them (2:12), had himself been comforted by news of their faith (3:7); now he provides them with reasons why they should be comforted (4:18; 5:11). When he turns to the church's role in its nurture, he beseeches his readers (5:12),[51] and he ends the letter with an adjuration (5:27): "I adjure you by the Lord that this letter be read to all the brethren." While Paul is like the moralists in adapting his persuasion to the situations he envisages, he is totally unlike them in the way he qualifies his persuasion by referring to God or Christ.[52] The difference is nowhere as clear as in the prayers. They serve a hortatory purpose and appear at strategic places in the letter.[53]

Ancient letter theory required that a writer express himself in exactly the same way he would have in person.[54] Since a letter was thought to reflect the character and personality of its writer, one had to be careful to write as though one were speaking to the reader.[55] At the same time, letters should be written in a style adapted to the circumstances and mood of their readers.[56] These requirements would be still more important in a letter such as 1 Thessalonians, which was to be read to a gathering of the church and which would therefore function in the same manner as a sermon. Paul wrote with

49. *Diamartyromai* (1 Thess. 4:6) is stronger than *martyromai* (2:12) and is intensified by the reference to God as an avenger. See G. Milligan, *St. Paul's Epistles to the Thessalonians* (London: Macmillan & Co., 1908), 51.

50. "Commanded" (RSV) may be too strong a translation for *parēngeilamen*. The cognate *parangelia* (RSV: "instructions") in 1 Thess. 4:2 is equivalent to *praeceptum* or *parangelma*, a precept on how to live in a particular situation. See Malherbe, "Exhortation in First Thessalonians," *NovT* 25 (1983): 250 n. 49.

51. *Erōtaō* ("beseech") is used with *parakaleō* in 1 Thess. 4:1, where they are synonymous and to be understood as an epistolary formula. For *erōtaō* in papyrus letters, see A. Deissmann, *Light from the Ancient East,* trans. L. R. M Strachan (reprint, Grand Rapids: Baker Book House, 1965), 168 n. 2; 179 n. 12; 193 n. 15. In 5:12, however, the use does not seem so formulaic.

52. See Malherbe, "Exhortation in First Thessalonians," *NovT* 25 (1983): 250–54.

53. 1 Thess. 1:2–3; 2:13; 3:11–13; 5:23. For the hortatory feature, see G. P. Wiles, *Paul's Intercessory Prayers,* SNTSMS 24 (Cambridge: Cambridge Univ. Press, 1974); cf. K. Stendahl, "Paul at Prayer," *Interpretation* 34 (1980): 240–49.

54. Cicero *Letters to His Friends* 2.4.1; Seneca *Epistle* 75.1.

55. See n. 24 above, and cf. Cicero *Letters to His Friends* 16.16.2. On a letter as speech in the written medium, see Cicero *Letters to Atticus* 8.14.1; 9.10.1; 12.53; Seneca *Epistle* 75.1.

56. Cicero *Letters to His Friends* 2.4.1; 4.13.1; *Letters to Atticus* 9.4.1.

the reception of the letter in mind (5:27).[57] Such consistency in the way one expressed oneself in person and in a letter was more easily maintained when the relationship between writer and reader remained cordial. It was not always possible for Paul to maintain the same demeanor in his letters that he had shown in person, for the circumstances in some of his churches changed rapidly and drastically. When this happened, as it did in Corinth, his critics accused him, in terms they derived from epistolographic theory, of inconsistency, as they did in the accusation Paul quotes in 2 Cor. 10:10: His letters are demanding and vigorous, but in person he is weak and his speech a round zero.

First Thessalonians, on the other hand, is remarkable for the pains Paul has taken to write a letter that reveals in detail the same character that he says he had displayed when he was with them. Separated from them in person but not in heart, Paul writes a letter designed to overcome the distance between them and continue what he had begun. They have not been abandoned, left to fend for themselves. Nor is their own knowledge so meager or their development so modest as to justify consternation or dismay. Rather, a firm base has been established on which they can build under the continuing guidance of Paul. Paul's great achievement in the letter lies not only in the way he strengthens his relationship with the Thessalonians but also in the success with which he has made a parenetic letter serve his pastoral purpose.[58] This is a distinctive contribution by Paul.

## THE NURTURING CONGREGATION

So far we have focused on Paul's efforts to continue nurturing the Thessalonians. Now we turn to examine the role of the Thessalonians themselves in continuing that nurture. The individuals who had become imitators of Paul had formed a community around him. While that community's relationship to Paul was of crucial importance to both Paul and them, Paul expected them to undertake their own

57. Note also the "health wish" in the closing of the letter (5:23–24), which has affinities (e.g., *holoklēros*) with those closings which look forward to the reception of the letter. See Koskenniemi, *Studien* (n. 5 above), 185–89, cf. 135.

58. For the pastoral purpose of 1 Thessalonians, see also von Dobschütz, *Die Thessalonicherbriefe* (chap. 2, n. 60), 20; Marxsen, *Der erste Brief* (n. 13 above), 24–25, 28.

nurture when he was not with them. Relationships within such groups (chapter 2) needed constant attention, and Paul had already instructed his converts on their relationship with one another (4:9-10). The communal interest pervades the letter and reflects Paul's concern to deepen his readers' understanding of the nature of the community they constituted, how they were to conduct themselves as members of it, and the ways in which they were to nurture one another.

## The Eschatological Community

Paul calls the Thessalonians a church (*ekklēsia*) only once in the letter, in the address, "To the church of the Thessalonians in God the Father and the Lord Jesus Christ" (1:1). In Paul's letters, *ekklēsia* usually refers to local assemblies, or congregations, as it does here.[59] The qualification of the assembly as "in God the Father," however, is unusual for Paul, and it is probable that "in" is to be understood instrumentally, that is, as indicating that the assembly was called into existence by God the Creator, who made them his family.[60] Then the sense would be the same as 1 Cor. 1:9, "you were called into the fellowship of his Son, Jesus Christ our Lord." The reference in 1:4 to the Thessalonians' election or call by God who loved them supports this interpretation, as do 2:12, "God, who calls you into his own kingdom and glory," and 5:24, "He who calls you is faithful, and he will do it" (that is, he will sanctify and preserve them at the coming of Christ).

It is this pervasive eschatological dimension in the letter that gives the Thessalonian community its special character. Paul's readers are not a ragtag group of manual laborers formed by an itinerant

59. On the view of the church in the letter, see Collins, *Studies* (chap. 2, n. 59), 58-63, 285-98.
60. See Best, *Commentary* (chap. 2, n. 57), 62. "Father" may here have the connotation of God as the source of all life, as it does in 1 Cor. 8:6, which reflects preaching to Gentiles. It was a favorite way of Philo to refer to God as creator—e.g., in *Special Laws* 1.41; 2.225; cf. *On Dreams* 2.178. In *Questions and Answers on Exodus* 2. 2, Philo writes of the proselyte, whose mind is alienated from polytheism and familiar with honoring one God and Father of the universe. Paul's reference to the "living God" in the outline of his preaching to the Thessalonians (1:9) shows that he spoke to them of the Creator, for "living God" conveyed that notion in Hellenistic-Jewish as well as Christian preaching to Gentiles. Cf. Acts 14:15. See pp. 30-32. On Paul's use of kinship language, see pp. 48-51 and R. Banks, *Paul's Idea of Community: The Early House Churches in Their Historical Setting* (Grand Rapids: Wm. B. Eerdmans, 1980), 52-61.

tentmaker. Rather, they are a community created and loved by God and occupy a special place in his redemptive scheme.[61] Paul is careful in other places in the letter, also, to characterize the community as not confined to this age. When he stands before the Lord at the parousia, he will boast of them (2:19). His prayer in 3:11–13, which forms a hinge for the two major sections of the letter, concludes with a petition for love among members of the community so that God "may establish your hearts unblamable in holiness before our God and Father, at the coming of our Lord Jesus with all his saints." And Paul's comforting parenesis in 4:13–17 is grounded in God's and Christ's actions which ensure the eternal constitution of the community: "God will bring with him those who have fallen asleep" (4:14); those still alive at the parousia "shall not precede those who have fallen asleep" (4:15); the living "shall be caught up together with them in the clouds to meet the Lord in the air; and so we shall always be with the Lord" (4:17). Even death is no threat to the community! This eschatological language, which "reinforces the sense of uniqueness and solidarity of the community,"[62] itself contains hortatory elements and also provides the perspective for the detailed advice Paul gives.

In view of this understanding of the church, note that all the items of conduct Paul takes up in the latter half of the letter in one way or another have relationships within the community in view. In his treatment of marriage, transgression is described as fraud of a Christian brother (4:6). Social responsibility is inculcated in a setting provided by brotherly love (4:9). The consoling description of the parousia is offered to enable the grieving Thessalonians to comfort one another (4:18). After an exhortation to live in expectation of the Day of the Lord, Paul again calls on them to encourage one another (5:11). Members of the community of the last days do not live solitary lives.

As Paul moves toward the end of the letter, he increasingly brings into view his readers' responsibility for their community's pastoral care. He does not want them to grieve over those who had fallen asleep, so he clarifies the hope they should have (4:13–17). But it is

---

61. Pax ("Beobachtungen zur Konvertitensprache im ersten Thessalonicherbrief," *Studii Biblici Franciscani Analecta* 21 [1971]: 234) has detected Jewish "conversion language" in Paul's reference to the Thessalonians as loved by God.

62. W. A. Meeks, "Apocalyptic Language" (chap. 2, n. 88), 694.

they, because of that hope, who are to comfort one another (4:18). With people in mind who, like the Epicureans, sought security in this life (5:3), he urges his readers to live in the light of the Day (5:1–10), but concludes: "Therefore encourage (*parakaleō*) one another and build (*oikodomeō*) one another up, just as you are doing" (5:11). It is as the community of the last days ("therefore") that they are to engage in pastoral care of one another. Paul's specifications of that care have become intensified. In addition to encouragement, he now mentions their edification. More significant is that they are to care for one another, literally, "one on one." As Paul, in the manner of the moral philosophers, had bestowed his attention on individuals and adapted his care to their needs,[63] so must the Thessalonians now, in effect, follow his example. Paul provides further details about the congregation's mutual exhortation in 5:12–15, to which 5:11 is a transition. The general statement on encouragement and edification then receives further explication.[64] What he then says in 5:12–15 has its counterpart in discussions about the ideal relationships between philosophers and their students, and especially between members of philosophic communities.

## Nurture Among the Philosophers

The social, intellectual, and psychological difficulties experienced by members of philosophic communities were addressed by a well-developed system of pastoral care known as psychagogy, which included what we mean by spiritual exercises, psychotherapy, and psychological and pastoral counseling.[65]

63. See pp. 56, 76. For the community's responsibility to individuals elsewhere in Paul, see Rom. 14:1; 15:1–6; 1 Cor. 4:6; 5:5; 8:7–13; 10:23–31; 11:17–33; 2 Cor. 2:5–11; Gal. 6:1–5; Phil. 4:2–3; 2 Thess. 1:3.

64. Commentators are, for the most part, content to relate 5:11 to what precedes. It is, however, directly related to what follows. See J. Hainz, *Ekklesia. Strukturen paulinischer Gemeinde-Theologie und Gemeinde-Ordnung* (Regensburg: Verlag Pustet, 1972), 42–47; Laub, *Eschatologische Verkündigung* (Introd., n. 2), 89–91.

65. For the conditions of members of the philosophic communities, see pp. 36–43. For psychagogy, in addition to Rabbow, *Seelenführung* (chap. 2, n. 6), and P. Hadot, *Exercices spirituels* (chap. 2, n. 6), see I. Hadot, *Seneca* (chap. 1, n. 60), esp. 39–78, 164–76; E. des Places, "Direction spirituelle. I. Dans l'antiquité classique," *Dictionnaire de Spiritualité* 3 (1957), 1002–8; H. G. Ingenkamp, *Plutarchs Schriften über die Heilung der Seele* (Göttingen: Vandenhoeck & Ruprecht, 1971); T. Bonhoeffer, *Ursprung und Wesen der christlichen Seelsorge*, BET 95 (Munich: Chr. Kaiser Verlag, 1985), 53–85, who is largely dependent on Rabbow.

## A Stoic

We have seen that Epictetus could be cutting in his treatment of his students, but he also guided them as their spiritual director. After lecturing on technical subjects, he would deal with the practical problems of the students in a less formal manner.[66] Not only did he instruct them in spiritual exercises and meditations that would prepare them to deal with the emotions that unsettled them but he also gave them advice on how to make moral progress by cultivating proper habits and evaluating their own lives. This evaluation took the form of a regimen of introspection throughout the day in which philosophical principles were applied to every circumstance and experience of the day.[67] Most of this instruction took place in the classroom, but Epictetus also recognized the value of private conferences.[68]

In addition to instruction aimed at them as individuals, Epictetus also gave directions that involved them as members of a group. The disciples were to read from the philosophers as a preparation for life with the conviction that their reading would lead them to virtue.[69] Those more experienced, who perhaps also served as tutors, pointed others to helpful readings. That this was not always done with consideration for the ability of the student to understand the reading is shown by Epictetus's reprimand of a senior student who had laughed at the performance of someone who had followed his advice.[70] This incident, as well as other comments by Epictetus, indicates that the students read such pieces to each other.[71]

Students were also encouraged to write moral literature for their own benefit and to read it to their fellows for their benefit and for comment by them.[72] The procedure is reflected in the following advice from Epictetus on how to prepare for exile:

66. See Stowers, *The Diatribe,* 53–58, for Epictetus's discourses or diatribes.
67. For Epictetus and his students, see Hijmans, *ASKESIS* (chap. 1, n. 60), 77–86, 92–102. For introspection, see Epictetus *Discourses* 1.4.20; 3.3.14–19; 3.8; 3.12; 3.24.84–94, and for the development of habits, *Discourses* 3.10.1–3; 4.6.34–35. The rules applied were memorized: *Discourse* 3.24.9.
68. Hijmans, *ASKESIS* (chap. 1, n. 60), 93–94.
69. Epictetus *Discourses* 1.4.9; 2.16.34; 4.4.11; cf. 1.4.5–17; contrast 3.24.38–39.
70. Epictetus *Discourse* 1.26.13. Tutors were to regard themselves as interpreters of the divine laws.
71. Epictetus *Discourse* 2.17.34–35.
72. Epictetus *Discourses* 3.26.3; 4.5.36.

Have thoughts like these ready at hand by night and by day; write them, read them, make your conversation about them, communing with yourself, or saying to another, "Can you give some help in this matter?" And again, go now to one man and now to another. Then, if some one of those things happens which are called undesirable, immediately the thought that it was not unexpected will be the first thing to lighten the burden.[73]

(Epictetus Discourse 3.24.103–4)

Even in a scholastic setting, then, we discover an expectation that members of the group would habitually engage in practices designed to contribute to each other's development. They would also carefully consider the conditions or abilities of those they were expected to help.

## A Platonist

Plutarch similarly recognized the value of encouragement of others in making moral progress. Some people, he says in his tractate *On Progress in Virtue,* are not dismayed by the slowness of their progress but are made to soar to new heights by the help they receive and by the strength and eagerness that come from what they in fact have accomplished.[74] That requires, however, a willingness to benefit from what they hear and see.[75] They are to pay close attention to the words and deeds of those who have made progress, fully aware that some people, who are themselves still neophytes, roughly assert themselves as they strive for prominence.[76] Respect for those whom one emulates is particularly important:

Indeed a peculiar symptom of true progress is found in this feeling of love and affection for the disposition shown by those whose deeds we try to emulate, and in the fact that our efforts to make ourselves like them are always attended by a goodwill which accords to them a fair meed of honour. But, on the other hand, if any man is imbued with a spirit of contentiousness and envy towards his betters, let him understand that he is merely chafing with jealousy at another's repute or power, but not honouring or even admiring virtue.[77]

(Plutarch Progress in Virtue 84E)

---

73. For the importance of premeditation, especially among the Stoics, see p. 57.
74. Plutarch *Progress in Virtue* 77B.
75. Plutarch *Progress in Virtue* 79D–F; 84B–85B.
76. Plutarch *Progress in Virtue* 80EF.
77. See the entire section, Plutarch *Progress in Virtue* 84B–85B.

Those desiring to make progress should be willing to accept correction, but Plutarch knows that people differ in their moral condition and that those who are worse off and most in need of reproof (*elenchos*) and admonition (*nouthesia*) are least likely to confess their sins.[78]

In view of the importance of what is involved, those who undertake the correction of others have special responsibilities. They must have a genuine desire to be of help, must be reasonable and mild rather than contentious, and make sure that their instruction is timely and adapted to the circumstances at hand.[79] It is a true friend who knows when to reprove and when to speak words of healing,[80] and Plutarch elsewhere deals at length with the frankness that is not only appropriate to but incumbent on friends.[81]

Plutarch's discussion of frankness in his tractate *How to Tell a Flatterer from a Friend* has much in common with the work of Philodemus, an Epicurean, *On Frankness,* which treats in detail the ways in which an Epicurean community was to engage in the nurture of its members.[82] It was the Epicureans who had developed the system of psychagogy, but what Philodemus says in the first century B.C. is reflected in the writings of Seneca, Paul's Stoic contemporary, and a generation later by the Platonist Plutarch. In short, the concerns and techniques that interest us were widespread at the time Paul wrote. The Epicureans, however, are of special interest, for, like Paul, they formed genuine communities that engaged in mutual exhortation.[83]

---

78. Plutarch *Progress in Virtue* 81F–82F.
79. Plutarch *Progress in Virtue* 80B–F.
80. Plutarch *Progress in Virtue* 82AB.
81. Plutarch *How to Tell a Flatterer from a Friend,* esp. 59A–74E.
82. Philodemus's *On Frankness* is the report of a speech made by his teacher, Zeno of Sidon. Only fragments of the work have been preserved (see p. 42 n. 29). The most important studies of it are: N. W. De Witt, "Organization and Procedure in Epicurean Groups," *CPh* 31 (1936): 205–11, which is still useful despite corrections suggested by M. Gigante, "Philodème: Sur la liberté de parole," *Actes du VIIIe Congrès, Assoc. Guillaume Budé* (Paris, 1969), 196–217; Rabbow, *Seelenführung* (chap. 2, n. 6), 269–70; Hadot, *Seneca* (chap. 1, n. 60), 63–67. Cf. also Schmid, "Epikur," *RAC* 5 (1962): 740–46; M. T. Riley, "The Epicurean Criticism of Socrates," *Phoenix* 34 (1980): 63–66.
83. On the Epicureans as a community rather than a school, see Clay, "Individual and Community" (chap. 2, n. 35), 265–66; cf. N. W. De Witt, "Epicurean *Contubernium,*" *TAPA* 67 (1936): 55–63.

## An Epicurean

The precise way in which the Epicurean communities were organized is still under dispute, but it is generally agreed that their members belonged to different ranks and that the more advanced members of the community had a special responsibility to nurture and admonish those of lesser standing. The basic principle that determined the nature of the community was friendship, which was to ensure the interdependence of members and a mutuality of concern on all levels. Philodemus thus addresses his comments on frank speech to both those who were doing the admonishing and those who received it.[84]

The leaders are to be the best of friends to the community and must speak out of goodwill and affection.[85] They must have a genuine desire to help their fellows by rescuing them from error and keeping them safe.[86] Actuated by the good of others, they must cultivate a correct disposition, which will keep them from hating those in error, for they will be conscious of their own shortcomings.[87] They will therefore not interpret others' misconduct as a personal affront but will strive to help them because they sympathize with them.[88] Their frankness will expose error but will vary its character as it is applied. As physicians take into consideration the proper time for certain cures and the conditions of their patients when they apply

84. From what follows, it would appear that Philodemus was especially concerned with the relationship between the leaders, who had attained an advanced state in their development, and junior members of the community, who were "in preparation." *On Frankness* VIIIa and VIIIb, however, suggest that he also may have had in mind the relationship between leaders themselves. Or, as Riley ("The Epicurean Criticism of Socrates," *Phoenix* 34 [1980]: 66) seems to think, these two fragments may deal with their reception of criticism from the membership at large. De Witt's sketch of the hierarchical structure of the Epicurean communities should not lead to the supposition that exhortation came only from the top. Reciprocity was regarded as intrinsic to friendship.

85. Philodemus *On Frankness* 41, 44, 61, Ib, II.

86. Helpers: Philodemus *On Frankness* 8, 18, 36, 67, 86. Saving from error: *On Frankness* 39, 40.

87. Disposition: Philodemus *On Frankness* Ia. Imperfection: 46, 56; cf. Plutarch *How to Tell a Flatterer from a Friend* 71EF.

88. Affront: Philodemus *On Frankness* 37, Ia. Sympathy: *On Frankness* 43, 79; cf. Plutarch *How to Tell a Flatterer from a Friend* 72AB.

them, so will responsible philosophers.[89] They will therefore not engage in unrelieved censure or insult, nor belittle those they seek to help, but will try to create in them a disposition to be benefited and will overcome their resistance.[90]

In order to be effective in adapting their exhortation, speakers will be sensitive to the different characters of those they wish to help.[91] They know that the young may be stiff-necked and easily irritated,[92] that they should be treated with gentleness to make them amenable to correction,[93] and that their capacity to endure reprimand must always be taken into consideration.[94] The strong and forceful in nature need frankness of a harsher kind, and those of an ugly disposition must be tamed by frankness.[95] Some covet honor and like to show off, and some are lazy and procrastinate,[96] but there are also some who are weak, who are not cured by frankness and may renounce philosophy.[97] If circumstances require, reproof will be public, straightforward, and direct, but Philodemus too recognizes the value of private instruction.[98] If the error is more complex, so must be the correction, which may then be compounded of reproof, praise, and exhortation.[99] Speakers should not give up quickly but should be patient in repeating their instruction.[100]

Those who receive admonition also have responsibilities. They are to reciprocate the goodwill of their teachers, who out of kindness

89. The varied character of *parrēsia:* Philodemus *On Frankness* 68, 86. The medical metaphor: *On Frankness* 22, 25, 37, 50, 63, 64, 69, 79, 84, XVIIa, XVIIb; cf. Plutarch *How to Tell a Flatterer from a Friend* 66A, 67EF, 73E, 74D. Also see Malherbe, "Medical Imagery" (chap. 1, n. 59), 19–35; idem, "'In Season and Out of Season': 2 Timothy 4:2," *JBL* 103 (1984): 235–43.
90. Philodemus *On Frankness* 13, 66, 79.
91. For Epicurus's classification of people, see Seneca *Epistles* 52.3; cf. 94.50–52; 95.36; Cicero *Tusculan Disputations* 4.32. For the psychological condition of the Epicurean converts, see pp. 41–43.
92. Philodemus *On Frankness* 31, 71.
93. Philodemus *On Frankness* 2, 8, 10.
94. Philodemus *On Frankness* 38.
95. Philodemus *On Frankness* 7, 86.
96. Philodemus *On Frankness* 34, V.
97. Philodemus *On Frankness* 59, cf. 7.
98. Public: Philodemus *On Frankness* 31, cf. 10. Private: *On Frankness* 8, 35, 53, VIIa. See chap. 2, n. 86.
99. Philodemus *On Frankness* 58, 68.
100. Philodemus *On Frankness* 64, 67, 69.

want to help them.[101] The students should therefore not be irritated when they are corrected, nor distrust their teachers.[102] Rather, as they submit to the treatment of physicians, so should they submit to the admonition of their teachers, who may similarly cause them pain.[103] They should not impugn the motives of their teachers, especially when they detect error in the ones who admonish. In such cases they should not retaliate by focusing on the shortcomings of the teacher, nor should they, when a particular admonition is in error, reject it on another occasion, when it is appropriate.[104] Their attitude should rather be one of gratitude.[105] They should also be willing to reveal their own shortcomings without waiting for the teacher to expose them, and they should be ready to confess their errors to their teacher as well as to their fellows.[106] The exhortation in the community was not to flow in one direction only, from the seniors to persons of lesser standing—both were open to correction.[107] The important thing was that they were friends who were genuinely concerned for each others' personal growth.

## Conclusion

This sampling of the psychagogy of a Stoic, a Platonist, and an Epicurean opens a window for us on the way in which people sought

101. Philodemus *On Frankness* 26, 31, 51–52, VIIIa, VIIIb.
102. Philodemus *On Frankness* 1, 31, 38.
103. Philodemus *On Frankness* 39, 42, 50, 63, 64, 69, 84.
104. Philodemus *On Frankness* 35, 56, 63. For the view that the philosopher should not retaliate, see esp. the Stoics contemporary with Paul: Seneca *On Anger* 1.16.1 and *On the Firmness of the Wise Man* 12.3; Musonius Rufus *Fragment* 10; Epictetus *Discourses* 3.22.54; 4.1.127 and *Encheiridion* 42; Dio Chrysostom *Discourse* 77/78.42; cf. A. C. van Geytenbeek, *Musonius Rufus and Greek Diatribe* (Assen: Van Gorcum, 1963), 134–42. See also Plutarch *How to Tell a Flatterer from a Friend* 72EF.
105. Philodemus *On Frankness* Xa, Xb, XIVb. Gratitude was sometimes expressed in financial contributions. See N. W. De Witt, "The Epicurean Doctrine of Gratitude," *AJP* 58 (1937): 324–27.
106. Philodemus *On Frankness* 39–46, 49, 53, 73. On confession, see S. Sudhaus, "Epikur als Beichtvater," *ARW* 14 (1911): 647–48; W. Schmid, "Contritio und 'ultima linea rerum' in neuen epikureischen Texten," *RhM* 100 (1957): 303–14. Philodemus's discussion reveals the psychological difficulties of baring one's soul and makes understandable his stress on the desirability of private instruction. That members of the community were urged to report each other's lapses (*On Frankness* 50) would only have raised the level of anxiety.
107. Philodemus *On Frankness* 75, XVIIIb. Cf. n. 84 above.

to help each other in a way of life different from that of the larger society. When groups are clearly in view, as with Epictetus and Philodemus, the responsibility of their various leaders receives close attention, but equally important is what is expected of the other members of the group. Whatever the group, and however it might be structured, they shared a concern for each other. Those who led in exhorting were to do so out of friendship and a genuine desire to help. Throughout the discussions there is a stress on the need to give close attention to the psychological condition of those they intended to help and to adapt their exhortation accordingly. The exhortation should always be timely, preferably in private and thus individualized, and conducted patiently, without expecting immediate success. The recipients are urged to receive admonition willingly, with love, affection, honor, and gratitude to those who wish to help them and not to be irritated and lash back at them.

## THE NURTURING CHURCH

Paul begins the last section of his letter with the same considerations in mind (5:12–15).[108] It is important to recognize that 5:11 introduces this section, for here (sc. 5:11) is to be observed the exercise of the pastoral duty by every member of the church, just as Paul claims to have taken fatherly concern for every individual (2:11).[109] Paul's own exhortations have had the church as a community in mind. Here he gives directions on how the community is to continue its own nurture.

Paul addresses two aspects of that pastoral care: the attitude toward those who exercise it (5:12–13) and the manner in which it is to be exercised (5:14–15). The interpretation of this passage has been bedeviled by attempts to discern in it the earliest New Testament evidence of the institutional organization of the church.[110] Paul does not,

---

108. The entire section (1 Thess. 5:12–22) deals with intracommunal relationships. However, the break marked by the exhortation to rejoice, pray, and give thanks (vv. 16–18) allows us to treat 5:12–15 as a unit.

109. E. von Dobschütz, *Christian Life in the Primitive Church,* trans. G. Bremner (New York: G. P. Putnam's Sons, 1904), 88.

110. The interpretation that follows has much in common with that of Hainz, *Ekklesia* (n. 64 above), 37–47; Laub, *Eschatologische Verkündigung* (Introd., n. 2), 85–95; idem, "Paulus als Gemeindegründer" (Introd., n. 2), 31–38. See also H. Greeven,

however, mention any particular office, nor does he have in mind two clearly defined groups, one that has assumed the responsibility for pastoral care and another that habitually receives it. His commands in 5:11, that the Thessalonians "encourage one another and build one another up," show that he has in mind their mutual nurturing. Rather than rigidly defined groups, Paul has in mind certain activities in which community members engage and the proper responses to them. He addresses both sets of considerations to the entire church (the "brethren"; 5:12, 14), as he has his other advice in the letter. We should keep in mind that this small church, made up largely of people converted from paganism, had been in existence less than a year. It would therefore be anachronistic to interpret this situation in the light of structures that developed gradually in other churches.

Paul begins his directions on the proper attitude toward those who exhort by beseeching his readers and ends by commanding them (5:12–13). That people engaging in pastoral care are to be respected and loved is, we have seen, also stressed in the moral philosophers' comments on pastoral care. So also is the warning against hostility. Paul's command that they be at peace with each other need therefore not imply that there was dissension in the church. It was in the nature of directions on frankness to anticipate some people's lack of openness to correction, and that is what Paul may be doing here.

Paul describes three aspects of the activity of the persons who should be respected and highly esteemed in love: "who labor among you and care for you in the Lord and admonish you" (v. 12). He explicitly provides a reason for the proper attitude toward them: their work. He also does so implicitly by specifying in each case that members of the congregation are the objects of their concern and that this care is exercised "in the Lord."

The personal interest of those who undertake pastoral care is further detailed in the affective description of two activities. Those to be loved "labor" (*kopiān*) among the Christians. *Kopos* conveys intense effort associated with tiredness (cf. 2:9). Paul uses it to describe his

"Propheten, Lehrer, Vorsteher bei Paulus. Zur Frage der 'Ämter' im Urchristentum," *ZNW* 44 (1952/53): 1–43, esp. 38–39; H. von Campenhausen, *Ecclesiastical Authority and Spiritual Power in the Church of the First Three Centuries,* trans. J. A. Baker (Stanford, Calif.: Stanford Univ. Press, 1969), 63–65.

apostolic work (3:5), and the word came to be used of others' evangelistic work.[111] Paul also uses it, however, of his own manual labor in 2:9. Either meaning is therefore possible in 5:12, but the two are not mutually exclusive.[112] What is significant for our immediate purpose is that Paul had already thanked God for the congregation's labor which was activated by love (1:3). That loving service is to be reciprocated in love.

The RSV translation for the second activity, "who are over you in the Lord" (*proistamenous*), is incorrect and is rejected by the vast majority of commentators. The verb *proistēmi* here describes caring for someone as it does in Rom. 12:8 and elsewhere.[113] The moral philosophers do not describe their pastoral care with these two terms, but the affectionate care with which their charges should be treated is a point stressed by Philodemus. Absent from Paul, on the other hand, is any statement about gratitude for benefits received. That would not express his understanding of pastoral work as grounded in faith (1:3), or care as engaged in "in the Lord." The work that is done is, in the final analysis, the work of the Lord.[114] That means the enterprise is viewed from a different perspective.

The third activity, admonition (*noutheteō*), frequently appears in discussions of exhortation. It is the only one of the three activities that also occurs in the section that treats the manner in which pastoral care is to be exercised (5:14–15). This section is similar in structure to the preceding one, beginning with an appeal and ending with an imperative, but otherwise it differs from the first set of

111. See A. von Harnack, "*Kopos* (*kopiän, hoi kopiōntes*) in frühchristlichen Sprachgebrauch," *ZNW* 27 (1928): 1–10.
112. Von Dobschütz (*Die Thessalonicherbriefe* [chap. 2, n. 60], 216) refers to Acts 20:35 but does not think that it can refer to pastoral care. However, Acts 20:18–35 is a summary portrayal of Paul's pastoral care. See Malherbe, "'Not in a Corner': Early Christian Apologetic in Acts 26:26," *The Second Century* 5 (1986). See R. M. Evans, "Eschatology and Ethics" (Diss., Basel University, 1967), 95–97, for the interpretation that a reaction developed against a "ministering element" which arose out of the artisan class. "Laborers" would therefore refer to their ministry as well as their daily manual labor.
113. Cf. 1 Tim. 3:4, 12, and the noun ("helper") used of Phoebe in Rom. 16:2. See, further, B. Reicke, "Proistēmi," *TDNT* 6 (1968): 700–703.
114. Hainz, *Ekklesia* (n. 64 above), 40: What Paul refers to here absolutely as *ergon* should be understood as *to ergon tou Christou* (cf. 1 Cor. 16:10; Phil. 2:30).

instructions. The four commands, to admonish (*noutheteō*), comfort (*paramytheomai*), help (*antechomai*), and be patient (*makrothymeō*), are not qualified theologically. The designation of the Thessalonians as "brethren" and the word used for being patient carry special Christian connotations,[115] but insofar as they reflect the communal context of the advice and enjoin patience, they are not out of the ordinary. With that qualification, the entire section, including the command not to retaliate, could as easily appear in Philodemus, Dio Chrysostom, or Plutarch.

Paul's main concern in this section is that the Thessalonians take care, as do responsible philosophic moralists, to match their styles of exhortation to the conditions of those whom they address. Paul begins with the injunction to admonish (*noutheteō*) the disorderly. A number of observations point to the significance of this type of exhortation in the situation Paul envisages. Admonition is the only type of exhortation Paul refers to in both sections, and here it stands at the head of the list. Furthermore, admonition is the harshest type of exhortation, whether his own or the Thessalonians', that Paul refers to in the letter.[116] In commanding them to admonish the disorderly, Paul thus wants them to be more forceful and demanding than he represents himself as having been. Admonition "is the instilling of sense in the person who is being admonished, and teaching him what should and should not be done."[117] It was sharp and vehement, and it made no effort to be palatable.[118] The natural reaction to it was hostility, and it tended to provoke people into responding in kind.[119] Nevertheless it was contrasted to faultfinding, and was not as harsh as

115. See J. Horst, "Makrothymia," *TDNT* 4 (1967): 375–87; A. Vögtle, *Die Tugend- und Lasterkataloge im Neuen Testament*, NTAbh 16 (Münster: Verlag Aschendorff, 1936), 154–55, 161 n. 11.

116. Admonition is stronger than Paul's insistence (2:12; 4:6) and directions (4:2, 11). Paul uses *nouthetein* of himself only in 1 Cor. 4:14 (cf. 19–21; Acts 20:31) and commands his readers to engage in it in 1 Thess. 5:14 and 2 Thess. 3:15 (cf. Rom. 15:14; 1 Cor. 10:11).

117. Pseudo-Demetrius *Epistolary Types* 7 (Malherbe, "Ancient Epistolary Theorists," *Ohio Journal of Religious Studies* 5 [1977]: 33). For the didactic element, cf. Dio Chrysostom *Discourse* 32.27. See also J. Behm, "Noutheteō, nouthesia," *TDNT* 4 (1967): 1019–22.

118. Dio Chrysostom *Discourses* 17.7; 32.10.

119. Dio Chrysostom *Discourses* 51.4, 7; 72.9–10; Plutarch *How to Tell a Flatterer from a Friend* 72EF.

reproof, reviling, blaming, abuse, or censure.[120] What distinguished it from these types of correction was the didactic element and the obvious concern to be helpful.[121] It was therefore not incongruous that it could be listed in conjunction with comforting, as Paul does.[122]

Admonition is the only type of exhortation that is to be addressed to persons who are not described in terms of their psychological condition but their behavior. In chapter 4 we shall discuss the issues that were at stake; here attention is drawn to the manner in which the church was to address the problem at this stage of the church's development. The RSV rendering of *ataktous* by "idle" is an interpretation rather than a translation. The verb and the adverb are used in 2 Thess. 3:6, 7, 11 of people who refuse to work, and in the papyri *ataktos* and its cognates are used interchangeably with idleness.[123] Paul does have in mind people who are not working (cf. 4:9–12), but the facile equation of idleness with *ataktos* obscures what is at issue. The word means "disorderly" and describes someone who does not submit to the accepted rules of life.[124] Idleness may be one way in which such a disposition is expressed, but by referring rather to some people as disorderly Paul draws attention to what he finds particularly disturbing—the social dimension of their disruptive behavior.[125] Paul had been relentless in his efforts to form and nourish the community. Conscious of the destructive effect that idleness could have within the community, and on its relationship to the larger society, he directs the community to be sharp in its admonition of those who threaten the fabric of its social relationships.

The next three admonitions have gentler treatment in mind and are more in harmony with his description of his own style of ministry. It is appropriate to comfort the fainthearted (cf. 2:11), perhaps those

120. Plutarch *How to Tell a Flatterer from a Friend* 66E. See Gerhard, *Phoinix von Kolophon* (chap. 1, n. 59), 35–39.

121. Plutarch *How to Tell a Flatterer from a Friend* 70DE and *How to Profit from One's Enemies* 89B; cf. Isocrates *Panegyricus* 130.

122. Cf. Plutarch *On Superstition* 168C.

123. See esp. Frame, *Epistles of St. Paul* (chap. 2, n. 56), 197.

124. See C. Spicq, "Les Thessaloniciens 'inquiets' étaient-ils des paresseux?" *ST* 10 (1956): 1–13.

125. Note also 2 Thess. 3:11. Cf. Bruce, *1 & 2 Thessalonians* (chap. 2, n. 56), 122–23.

who grieved over the Christians who had died (4:13) or those who were unable to take insults or endure trials.[126] The weak to be helped are most likely persons not up to the challenge of the moral life without the encouraging care of others.[127] Perhaps it is so difficult to identify the people who are to be comforted and helped because Paul did not have in mind particular groups in Thessalonica but rather conditions. That was the interest of writers who commented on pastoral care, as Paul does here. And, as we have seen, Philodemus also encouraged speakers in his community to be patient.

The moralists also warned against retaliation, as Paul does. Paul's warning, however, comes after he has enjoined comfort, help, and patience, which are unlikely to evoke a response that might cause a speaker to want to retaliate. That is striking. It is further striking that the command not to retaliate is directed to the speakers rather than to the people to whom they speak, as one would expect. We should remember that those who admonish were themselves new to the faith. Plutarch spoke of the tendency of neophytes to be rough and self-assertive, and Paul may have been aware of the same tendency in his converts. He therefore first speaks of admonition but then stresses the more caring types of exhortation to impress on them the necessity of aiding others by adapting to their needs. That he ends the section with a command not to retaliate, however, suggests that he is most concerned about the response to admonition. Admonition could easily cause hostility, especially toward people who were themselves novices without any official standing in the church. To such hostility the speaker in turn might be inclined to retaliate. Paul may be anticipating such a reaction and therefore directs his readers to be encouraging, supportive, and patient, but he also alerts them to beware of the natural tendency to strike back when they meet with hostility. He either knew that idleness was a problem in the church or suspected that it might become a problem. The speakers

126. Cf. Rigaux, *Aux Thessaloniciens* (chap. 2, n. 60), 584. For the latter, see John Chrysostom *Homilies on First Thessalonians,* Homily 10 (PG 62.457).

127. Spicq, "Les Thessaloniciens 'inquiets' étaient-ils des paresseux?" *ST* 10 (1956): 10 n. 6. Cf. Philodemus's concern for the weak. See also D. A. Black, "The Weak in Thessalonica: A Study in Pauline Lexicography," *JETS* 25 (1982): 307–21. Black thinks they were persons who were worried about the delay of the parousia.

who admonish the idle should, like the good philosophers, pursue the good of the community and of all people.[128]

## CONCLUSION

First Thessalonians reveals how the nurture of the community continued in Paul's absence. Timothy was sent to establish the Thessalonians in the faith and to ascertain whether they still looked to Paul for the pattern of their lives. Upon learning that they did, Paul writes a parenetic letter that serves a pastoral purpose. The letter continues the style of ministry in which Paul had engaged when he was with them. He impresses on them that they are a community of a special kind, that they are to conduct themselves accordingly, and that they are to engage in the same kind of exhortation and in the same manner that he had. The only difference is that they are to admonish those who threaten harmony within the community and jeopardize relationships with outsiders by their irresponsible, disorderly lives. Paul may be absent, but the nurture continues. As he had followed Greek and Roman precedents in shaping the church, in describing his own psychagogy, and in his adoption of the parenetic style, so he makes use of Greek and Roman traditions when he instructs the community how to continue that nurture.

128. Note also 1 Thess. 5:20, the negative evaluation of prophetic speech. The connection between Paul's advice in 5:14–15 and the activity of Christian prophets deserves more attention.

# 4

# The Christian
# Community
# in a Pagan Society

So far we have concentrated on Paul's efforts to ensure that the Thessalonians continued to grow as individuals within their Christian community. Paul does not, however, only direct their attention inward. Groups such as the Thessalonians could not exist without defining their relationship to the larger society. Thus 1 Thessalonians exhibits an interest in how the recently converted Christians were to conduct themselves toward outsiders. The Thessalonians' social conduct was of the greatest importance to Paul, so much so that he reserves admonition for those who are disorderly (5:14). In order to grasp the significance of his advice, we must determine what Paul perceived to be the major issue in the Christian community's relationship to its society.

In scattered statements throughout the letter, Paul reveals an ambiguous attitude toward Gentile non-Christians. On the one hand, he has a negative view of them. They are idolaters (1:9) and, without knowledge of God, are lustful (4:5). They have no hope (4:13), and as Jews had opposed him (2:16; cf. 2:2?), so Gentiles had caused the Thessalonians to suffer (2:14). Nevertheless, Christians are to love all people as they love each other (3:11–12) and should not repay evil with evil but seek to do good to all as they do to each other (5:15). The Christians' love and concern for non-Christians is, in effect, an extension of the care they have for each other. Although Paul is most interested in intracommunal relationships in his letter, nevertheless the ethic he teaches takes into consideration the Christians' attitude toward the larger society.[1]

## PAUL AND THE PHILOSOPHIC TEACHING ON THE QUIET LIFE

Paul gives his most explicit instruction regarding the need for Christians to lead a quiet life in 1 Thess. 4:9–12:

> But concerning love of the brethren you have no need to have any one write to you, for you yourselves have been taught by God (*theodidaktoi*) to love one another; and indeed you do love all the brethren throughout Macedonia. But we exhort you, brethren, to do so more and more, to aspire (*philotimeisthai*) to live quietly (*hēsychazein*), to mind your own affairs (*prassein ta idia*), and to work with your hands, as we charged you; so that you may command the respect of outsiders, and be dependent on nobody.

Like the other two places where he encourages a positive attitude toward non-Christians (3:11–12; 5:15), this passage begins with a reference to love within the community but concludes with a statement on the purpose of Paul's advice—"so that you may command the respect of outsiders, and be dependent on nobody." This passage contains more elements derived from the Hellenistic moralists than any other part of the letter. It abounds with parenetic features: "you have no need to have any one write to you"; "you yourselves have been taught by God"; "indeed you do love all the brethren"; "do so more and more"; "as we charged you"; and "we exhort you." Moreover, the passage contains terms derived from philosophic discussions of political and social conduct, which suggests that Paul fashioned an ethic that would be intelligible in such a context.

The items clearly derived from such discussions are his instructions: that his readers aspire to live quietly, that they mind their own affairs, and that they be self-sufficient (literally, "and have need of no one," or "of nothing"). The contrast between being meddlesome or being a busybody and living quietly and minding one's own affairs had frequently been taken up in discussions about Greek social and political

1. See W. C. van Unnik, "Die Rücksicht auf die Reaktion der Nicht-Christen als Motiv in der altchristlichen Paränese," in *Sparsa Collecta*, NovTSup 30 (Leiden: E. J. Brill, 1980), 307–22.

values before Plato.[2] Plato himself commended the person who "remains quiet (*hēsychazein*) and minds his own affairs (*ta hautou prattein*)," and characterized justice as minding one's own business and not being a meddler or busybody (*polypragmonein*).[3] The expression "to remain quiet and mind one's own business" came to describe the person who withdrew from the political arena, particularly in the late Roman Republic and early Empire, when renunciation of public life was a particularly attractive choice for thoughtful people.[4]

Living quietly or in retirement, however, met with severe criticism. Seneca reflects one such reason for criticism when he advises Lucilius to retire unostentatiously, "for what one avoids one condemns."[5] Seneca, a Stoic, considered retirement an opportunity for meditation and preparation for renewed activity, and in justification of his own retirement could refer to the founders of the Stoic school, who had themselves sent no one into public life. Plutarch, an aristocratic Platonist, totally disagreed. When Stoics argued in that way, he charged, they were socially irresponsible and, moreover, inconsistent, for they were assiduous in pursuing every possible opportunity to defraud their students.[6]

Agonizing over whether to live quietly was not confined to Stoics. The letters of Chion of Heraclea, dating from the latter half of the first century, represent no particular school, even though the writer does claim to be a friend of Plato. Nor does Chion show any originality of thought; he is, rather, representative of the widespread debate over the relative merits of the contemplative and practical ways of life. In one of his letters he celebrates friendship as a divine gift and describes his yearning for quietness in the company of his friend:

2. See V. Ehrenberg, "Polypragmosyne: A Study in Greek Politics," *JHS* 67 (1947): 46–67; A. W. H. Adkins, *Polupragmosune* and 'Minding One's Own Business': A Study in Greek Social and Political Values," *CPh* 71 (1976): 301–27. Much of the material from writers representing the popular morality is collected by F. Wilhelm, "Plutarchos Peri Hesychias," *RhM* 73 (1924): 466–82.

3. Plato *Republic* 496D, 433A.

4. Cf. Dio Cassius *Roman History* 60.27. For the temptation, especially among Stoics, to withdraw from active participation in society, see R. MacMullen, *Enemies of the Roman Order: Treason, Unrest and Alienation in the Empire* (Cambridge: Harvard Univ. Press, 1966), chap. 2. See also A.-J. Festugière, *Personal Religion Among the Greeks* (Berkeley and Los Angeles: Univ. of Calif. Press, 1954), chap. 4.

5. Seneca *Epistle* 14.8; cf. *Epistles* 56; 68; 73.

6. Plutarch *On Stoic Self-Contradictions* 1043A–1044B.

I had thus such a natural bent for a quiet life (*pros hēsychian*) that even as a young man I despised everything that could lead to an active and disturbed life. When I was settled in Athens, I did not take part in hunting, nor did I go on shipboard to the Hellespont with the Athenians against the Spartans, nor did I imbibe such knowledge as makes men hate tyrants and kings, but I associated with a man who is a lover of a quiet life and I was instructed in a most godlike doctrine. The very first precept of his was: seek stillness. For that is the light of philosophy, whereas politics and meddlesomeness wrap it in gloom and make the way to philosophy hard to find for those who search.[7]

(Chion of Heraclea *Epistle* 16.5)

Like Seneca, Chion too is aware that retirement may lead to an indolence that would make him unfit for a life of action, yet he persists in stressing the personal growth that quietness had made possible: he had learned to practice justice, had acquired self-control, and had learned to know God.[8]

These examples demonstrate that the language Paul uses to instruct the Thessalonians in social responsibility was commonly used in the first century to describe the contemplative life in opposition to an activism that was described as meddlesomeness (*polypragmosynē*). There are obvious differences, however, between Paul and these philosophers. Where Paul resembles the Stoics and persons like Chion is in his command to the Thessalonians "to live quietly" and "to mind your own affairs." Where he differs is in his expectation that by so doing his readers would meet with the approval of non-Christians ("outsiders," 1 Thess. 4:12). Furthermore, while the philosophers' retirement was to be filled with contemplation and cultivation of personal growth, the Thessalonians were to spend their time in manual labor, which introduces yet another problem, for manual labor was held in low esteem and unlikely to commend them to persons of some social standing.[9] Finally, Paul's concentration on manual labor and self-sufficiency shows that he is concerned with Christian behavior on the economic and social levels rather than on the political level, as was primarily the case with the philosophers we have so far encountered.

---

7. Chion, according to the translation of I. Düring, *Chion of Heraclea: A Novel in Letters* (Gothenburg: Wettergren & Kerbers, 1951), 75. Cf. *Epistle* 5.
8. Chion *Epistle* 16.6–8; cf. Seneca *Epistle* 56.9–10.
9. For the low evaluation of artisans, see Hock, *Social Context* (chap. 1, n. 40), 35–36.

Thus, while it is clear that Paul uses current language to advocate particular behavior, it is not yet clear why he does so, nor why he felt it necessary to comment on the Thessalonians' manual labor as the way they were to commend themselves to non-Christians.

## CHRISTIAN AND CYNIC IRRESPONSIBILITY

In attempting to gain clarity on Paul's use of this philosophic tradition, recall that he had founded the church as he worked at his trade to support himself. Gathering his converts around him, he had given them an example to follow. His purpose in doing so emerges from 2 Thessalonians. When he had not burdened them by demanding that they support him, it is said, it was not because he did not have the right to do so.

> For you yourselves know how you ought to imitate us; we were not idle (*ouk ētaktēsamen*) when we were with you, we did not eat any one's bread without paying, but with toil and labor we worked night and day, that we might not burden any of you. It was not because we have not that right, but to give you in our conduct an example to imitate. For even when we were with you, we gave you this command: If any one will not work, let him not eat. For we hear that some of you are living in idleness (*ataktōs*), mere busybodies, not doing any work. Now such persons we command and exhort in the Lord Jesus Christ to do their work in quietness (*meta hēsychias*) and to earn their own living.
>
> (2 Thess. 3:7–12)

Paul's own labor was paradigmatic when he established the church; it is referred to in 1 Thess. 2:9 where it provides the basis for his exhortation to the Thessalonians to work, and it occurs again in 2 Thessalonians. This sequence suggests a familiarity with a tendency among Paul's converts to abandon their occupations and to become busybodies. It is most likely this tendency that he has in mind in 1 Thess. 5:14 and for which he reserves admonition. That he was not successful, despite these efforts, in diverting some of the Thessalonians from becoming idle demonstrates the strength of the tendency. And that he brings outsiders (1 Thess. 4:12) into the discussion further suggests that the problem was not perceived as purely intracommunal.

By now widening our focus we may see more clearly what is involved. We have seen that Paul's method of centering his teaching in the workshop had precedents among some philosophers and that it was not unusual for the biographic tradition about philosophers to associate them with craftsmen and tradesmen.[10] Those philosophers, however, represented an ideal. The picture sketched by such commentators on society as Lucian of Samosata is much less flattering. The people Lucian had in mind were the Cynics who crowded the streets and squares, who had no training in philosophy but sought to escape their laborious trades by heeding the call to preach. Lucian describes the newfound freedom from social restraints that such Cynics touted and then comments, in his usual satirical manner:

> You shall see what will happen presently. All the men in workshops will spring to their feet and leave their trades deserted when they see that by toiling from morning till night, doubled over their tasks, they merely eke out a bare existence from such wage earning, while idle frauds live in unlimited plenty, asking for things in a lordly way, getting them without effort, acting indignant if they do not, and bestowing no praise even if they do.[11]
>
> (Lucian *The Runaways* 17)

To Lucian, laziness was obviously an important motive for adopting the "philosophic" life.

Lucian also levels another common criticism against the Cynics when he accuses them of meddlesomeness or busybodiness, the exact opposite of living quietly and tending to one's own affairs. He pillories the social irresponsibility of such preachers when he allows the Cynic who meddles in other people's affairs, but does no good in either public or private life, to speak for himself. In response to a question about what he contributes to society, the Cynic answers,

> I hold it unnecessary to be a merchant or a farmer or a soldier or to follow a trade; I shout, go dirty, take cold baths, walk about barefoot in winter, wear a filthy mantle and like Momus carp at everything the others do.
>
> (Lucian *Icaromenippus* 31)

Lucian represents the popular view of Cynics: they leave their jobs, sponge off people, contribute nothing to society, and meddle in other people's business. How common the criticism was appears from the

10. See pp. 18–20.
11. Cf. Lucian *Philosophies for Sale* 11.

manner in which even philosophers of a serious sort felt obliged to make the point that they were not busybodies but had a higher calling.[12] Dio Chrysostom illustrates the difficulty they faced. In the introduction to one of his speeches, he justifies his abandonment of normal pursuits. In fact, as a philosopher he

> goes about as neither farmer nor trader nor soldier nor general, nor as shoemaker or builder or physician or orator, nor as one engaged in any other customary occupation, but, on the other hand, comes and goes in this strange fashion and puts in an appearance in places where impulse or chance may lead him.[13]
>
> (Dio Chrysostom *Discourse* 80.1)

Dio's contention, that by abandoning normal occupations he did not become a meddler, but demonstrated the freedom which justified his philosophic frankness, was not likely to satisfy someone like Lucian.

This context, in which the newly converted abandoned their trades and took to the streets, helps to explain Paul's preoccupation with his own and his converts' employment. Aware of the criticism by members of polite society that such persons were disgraceful and socially irresponsible, busybodies who meddled in the affairs of others, Paul offered a contrary example in his own life. Whether or not this was the reason why he centered his activity in the workshop in the first place cannot be determined. That he did so, however, enabled him to be more forceful in his directions. By giving his instructions in terms that had come to be used of philosophers who sought a higher good by living quietly and avoiding meddlesomeness, Paul implicitly distanced Christians from the socially irresponsible Cynics.

## CHRISTIANS AND EPICUREAN IRRESPONSIBILITY

There is yet another difference between Paul's directions and the situation of those retirement-seeking philosophers described so far in this chapter. Chion retired in the company of a friend, but none of the others emphasize such an association or make any mention of a community of kindred souls. Paul, by contrast, considers his directions to

12. Epictetus *Discourse* 3.22.95–97; cf. 81–85.
13. Cf. Dio Chrysostom *Discourse* 31.2–3; cf. Maximus of Tyre *Discourse* 15.9.

fall under the heading of brotherly love (1 Thess. 4:9), that is, the special relationship within the Christian community. He uses the term "brotherly love" (*philadelphia*) only once elsewhere, in Rom. 12:10, where he instructs his readers to be affectionate toward one another in brotherly love. That he has in mind more than mere affection, however, appears from Rom. 12:13, in the same context: "Contribute to the needs of the saints, practice hospitality." For Paul, as for other writers in the New Testament, brotherly love showed a practical concern for the material needs of members of the church (cf. Heb. 13:1–3; 1 Pet. 4:8–9) and in Thessalonica he was sensitive to the possibility that readiness to help those in need would be abused.

There was at least one philosophical community that also related its quietism to the friendship which gave it its character, namely, the Epicureans. Some salient features of the Epicurean school will cast further light on Paul's instructions. Epicureans believed that their security or happiness (*eudaimonia*) derived from a quiet life (*hēsychia*) and retirement from the world (*lathe biōsas*) and they therefore freed themselves from the prison of public life and politics.[14] Organized as a community of friends, they claimed not to be ambitious for honor or praise from those outside their community. Their low esteem for normal pursuits included a rejection of education in the liberal arts—an attitude that had been exemplified by Epicurus himself, who fostered the reputation that he was self-taught. They were concerned for their friends and advocated financial support for one another. A widespread view of friendship in antiquity was that friends held all things in common, but Epicurus had considered this improper on the grounds that it implied mistrust and placed no confidence in the help that was available in friends. The fragments of his letters that have been preserved contain numerous requests for assistance for himself and for other members of the community. In seeking such support, he aimed at balance, as one saying attributed to him indicates:

> He is no friend who is continually asking for help, nor he who never associates help with friendship. For the one barters kindly feeling

14. Epicurus *Principal Doctrine* 14; Vatican Collection 58. See p. 43.

for a practical return and the other destroys the hope of good in the future.[15]

(Vatican Collection 39)

Philodemus also discusses at some length the occupations considered fit for a philosopher and ends as follows:

> To derive one's means from the breeding of horses is ridiculous, from the exploitation of mines by servile labor unenviable, from those two sources by working oneself, pure madness. Miserable also is the lot of the farmer who works with his own hands. "But," says he, "to live off the land while others farm it—that is truly in keeping with wisdom. For then one is least entangled in business, the source of so many annoyances; there is indeed found a becoming way of life, a withdrawal into leisure with one's friends, and for those who moderate their desires, the most honorable source of revenue."[16]

(Philodemus *On Household Management* 23)

Philodemus's attitude toward manual labor is clearly that of a favored class, but it could only contribute to the opinion that Epicureans were indolent and regarded work as an impediment to a quiet life.

To the common mind, the Epicureans were the prime example of people who had abandoned public life. The attitude of Plutarch, the apostle of *philanthrōpia,* as he has been called,[17] is instructive. Aware that his readers might regard his *ad hominem* attack on the Epicureans as unfair, he justifies himself by claiming that he is representing the popular view of Epicureans. He rejects their claim that their quietism was a demonstration of friendship and strings together a series of accusations frequently leveled at them:

> But if celebrity is pleasant, the want of it is painful; and nothing is more inglorious than want of friends, absence of activity, irreligion, sensuality, and indifference—and such is the reputation of their sect among all mankind, except for themselves.[18]

(Plutarch *That Epicurus Makes a Pleasant Life Impossible* 1100CD)

15. Cf. Frischer, *Sculpted Word* (chap. 2, n. 18), 43–45. On financial gifts within the Epicurean communities, see De Witt, "The Epicurean Doctrine of Gratitude," *AJP* 58 (1937): 324–27; Westman, *Plutarch gegen Kolotes* (chap. 2, n. 28), 225–27.
16. Translation by Festugière, *Personal Religion* (n. 4 above), 56.
17. R. Hirzel, *Plutarch* (Leipzig: Dieterich, 1912), 25.
18. For a Stoic's concern about inertia and hard work while in retirement, see Seneca *Epistle* 56.8–9.

This opinion of the Epicureans presents a problem in our attempt to understand how Paul used the philosophic traditions in his instructions to the Thessalonians. We have seen that he was aware of a tendency among converts to abandon their jobs. Many Cynics also did so and were regarded as busybodies who engaged in disgraceful behavior. Paul tried to counter this tendency among his converts by using language from the philosophic tradition which described the philosopher as one who retires and minds his own business. Paul's interest in individuals as members of a community is paralleled in the Epicurean school, the example par excellence of people who had withdrawn as a community from society. Paul's advice, therefore, might have sounded Epicurean.[19] But since the Epicureans were attacked for their social and political policy, how could Paul expect his advice to meet with the goodwill of non-Christians? It is possible that he was not aware of being "Epicurean" in his advice, or, if he was, that he simply did not care.

A number of features in the passage, however, suggest that he not only knew the Epicurean attitude but consciously sought to distinguish Christians from the Epicureans as well as the Cynics. To begin with, Paul does not speak of friends or friendship but of brotherly love (*philadelphia*). He was familiar with the conventional discussions about friendship but studiously avoided using the word itself.[20] The plausible suggestion has been made that he did so because of the anthropocentric connotations that "friend" carried among the Greeks (*philos*) and Romans (*amicus*), whereas he thought that Christian relationships were determined by God (cf. 4:9).[21]

When Paul says that the Thessalonians were taught by God (*theodidaktoi*) to love one another (1 Thess. 4:9), he further distinguishes them from the Epicureans. This is the first time *theodidaktos* appears in Greek literature, and Paul may well have coined it especially for this context in which he wishes to describe brotherly love as a divine teaching. Placed in the Epicurean context, the sig-

19. Seneca, also, was aware that by advising Lucilius to live quietly he might appear to be giving the same advice as Epicurus. Cf. *Epistle* 68.10.

20. See, e.g., Betz, *Galatians* (chap. 3, n. 37), 220–33.

21. J. N. Sevenster, "Waarom spreekt Paulus nooit van vrienden en vriendschap?" *NTT* 9 (1954/55): 356–63.

nificance of Paul's coinage becomes more evident. Epicurus had claimed to be self-taught (*autodidaktos*).[22] Paul's word, "God-taught," sounds as if it might be a conscious rejection of something that is "self-taught." Furthermore, the Epicurean view of friendship was criticized for being utilitarian, that it was prompted by need. Epicureans themselves were charged with being devoid of philanthropy and untouched by any spark of the divine.[23] Stoics, on the other hand, held that friendship sprang from nature and was a divine gift.[24] By saying that brotherly love was divinely taught, Paul would therefore subtly share such criticism of the Epicureans. But, as is clear from the self-description of himself as God's spokesman in 1 Thessalonians 1 and 2, the divine teaching he has in mind is not the natural endowment or aptitude that the Stoic thinks of as a divine gift, but is Paul's own teaching.

The most obvious difference between Paul and the Epicureans lies in their respective attitudes toward society. Epicureans shunned society in a manner that observers perceived as contemptuous. Paul's entire discussion, on the other hand, is aimed at earning the respect of society by promoting self-sufficiency ("so that you may . . . have need of no one [or nothing]"). His view of brotherly love is not utilitarian; on the contrary, brotherly love requires that the Thessalonians not burden each other but be self-sufficient. If they followed his advice, then they would be imitating him, for out of love for them he had supported himself (2:8–9). Nor does Paul conceive of the Christian community as a conventicle that isolates itself from the rest of society, deep in contemplation while gentlemen farmers provide the necessities of life.

The Epicureans disclaimed any political or social ambition and regarded their retirement as a demonstration of this lack of ambition.[25] Paul may have had this "lack of ambition" in mind when he tells the Thessalonians to aspire—literally, to make it their ambition (*philotimeisthai*)—to live quietly. This statement is paradoxical: his

22. Cf. Cicero *De Finibus* 1.71; Festugière, *Epicurus and His Gods* (chap. 1, n. 88), 34; *M. Tulli Ciceronis De Natura Deorum*, ed. A. S. Pease (Cambridge, Mass.: Harvard Univ. Press, 1955), 1.381–82.
23. Plutarch *That Epicurus Actually Makes a Pleasant Life Impossible* 1098DE.
24. Cf. Cicero *On Friendship* 19–20, 27; Seneca *Epistle* 9.17.
25. See p. 43. Cf. Plutarch *On Tranquility of Mind* 465F–466A.

readers are to be ambitious, but their "ambition" is to be exhibited in their quietness.[26] Furthermore, the quietness Paul has in mind is not an Epicurean withdrawal from society but the quiet pursuit of the Christians' ordinary lives. Paul is dealing with manual laborers who have a tendency not to live quietly but to interfere in other people's business. He wants them to be responsible members of society in a manner that would be recognized as appropriate to their social status. That differentiates him from the Epicureans and explains why he thought that his direction to lead a quiet life would meet with society's approval.[27]

This interpretation of Paul's advice would be speculative were it not for the fact that Christians continued to show an almost Epicurean avoidance of publicity. To an outsider, the Christian and Epicurean minority groups in many respects would appear similar: they were both regarded as atheistic, misanthropic, socially irresponsible, and sexually immoral. It is not surprising that their opponents sometimes mentioned them in the same breath.[28] In 1 Thessalonians, the earliest Christian writing we have, we see that Paul was alert to the similarities between the groups, yet sought to register their differences as he helped define the church's relationship to the larger society.

## CONCLUSION

We have now come full circle. We began this study by noting that Paul described his ministry in Thessalonica in terms derived from

---

26. Cf. Seneca's preoccupation with ambition while in retirement: *Epistle* 56.9–10.

27. I am indebted to Susan Garrett for pressing me to sharpen my earlier suggestions about Paul's awareness of the Epicureans' social attitudes. See Malherbe, *Social Aspects* (chap. 1, n. 5), 24–28; idem, "Exhortation in First Thessalonians," *NovT* 25 (1983): 252–54. The interpretation I offer differs markedly from that of many commentators who hold that Paul's instructions were necessitated by an expectation of the imminent parousia which led them to cease working. It need only be pointed out that Paul makes no connection between his readers' eschatological views and their idleness. In fact, with the exception of the statement that the Thessalonians were taught by God, the passage is remarkably free of theological elements. The issue was, in the first instance, a social rather than a theological one for Paul. Furthermore, Paul's references to his own labor when he had been with them (2:9) and his instruction to them on the matter at that time (4:11) show that he had been concerned about a potential problem before his converts could have fallen prey to idleness because they misunderstood his teaching.

28. For the avoidance of publicity, see p. 12 n. 29; for the similarities, see Malherbe, *Social Aspects*, 26 n. 61.

descriptions of the ideal philosopher. Such descriptions distinguished true philosophers from morally and socially irresponsible proclaimers of freedom such as the Cynics. Paul had a practical reason for making the distinction, for Cynics also were associated with the working class. An important distinction between Paul and Cynics, however, was Paul's effort to form and nurture a community. In this chapter we have seen that Paul is at great pains to keep his recent converts from adopting the Cynic way of life. And, once again, it is their relationship to other members of the community that provides the perspective for their relationship to the larger society: it is as they love each other and work to support themselves that they will gain the respect of outsiders. Paul is adept in using philosophic traditions when he clarifies for his readers what their attitude toward outsiders should be. He had been equally adept when instructing them on their nurture of each other.

Of special interest is the way in which the Christians' social responsibility and attitude toward the larger society are a part of Paul's and the community's nurturing concern. Indeed, if intensity were to be taken as the major criterion for measuring importance, admonition of the disorderly idlers would have been the most important in Paul's estimation. Social stability was, if not indispensable, then at least most desirable for the internal life of the church. While we have here focused, as Paul does, on how the Thessalonians' behavior might impress outsiders, in 2 Thess. 3:6–13 the concern is with the effect of idleness on the Christian community itself. When even admonition did not bring about responsible behavior, disruptive idlers would be denied the association of the church (2 Thess. 3:14–15). By thus establishing limits to its fellowship, the church would go considerably beyond admonition.

# Conclusion

We have examined one of Paul's letters for evidence of the way he founded a church and guided it during the first months of its life. First Thessalonians has proved to be an excellent source for this dimension of Paul's work. Written less than a year after he first entered Thessalonica, it reflects more clearly than any other of Paul's letters his method of forming a Christian community among Greek manual laborers. The events are fresh in Paul's mind and his letter reveals sympathetic insight into problems Greeks faced when they first became Christians. We should be careful, however, not to generalize about Paul's pastoral method on the basis of this one letter; it offers only one slice of his work. The conditions in Paul's churches could change rapidly and drastically, either because of internal or local factors or because traveling Christians from elsewhere might unsettle the churches Paul had left behind. Paul's other letters are addressed to such circumstances, and they reveal Paul's pastoral ability to match his style to the situations at hand. Nevertheless, 1 Thessalonians is valuable for what it tells us about the beginnings of a Greek church before external problems intruded.

The intention of this book has not been to make Paul a moral philosopher but to illuminate his practice by comparing it to that of his contemporaries who were engaged in a similar, if not identical, enterprise. We have seen that in many respects Paul's methods had their counterparts in those of the philosophers. The workshop as a semiprivate setting in which to discourse and bring his listeners to conversion, the presentation of himself as a model to be imitated, and his adaptation to the psychological conditions of individuals while trying to retain his own integrity represented the ideal to many of Paul's contemporaries. Paul consciously used the conventions of his day in attempting to shape a community with its own identity, and he did so with considerable originality. Thus, when he instructed the Thessalonians on their relationship to non-Christians, he showed a familiarity with the social attitudes of and toward philosophic converts. He was also careful to position the Christian community in the larger society. And when he was separated from them he adopted the convention of writing a letter, but he put a traditional hortatory style to a new, pastoral use. Throughout, Paul created the impression that he had been consistent in his teaching, demeanor, and relationship with the fledgling church.

In some respects, Paul was different from the moralists. Whereas even the most moderate philosophers claimed that it was necessary to be harsh at times, Paul represents himself as consistently mild in manner and speech. Furthermore, he sketches a picture of himself as self-giving out of love for his converts. That would have appeared to the philosophers as dangerously close to compromising one's integrity. At the same time, in describing his own practice, Paul claims for himself what was regarded as the ideal. He is also more confident in offering himself as a model to be imitated. But in doing so, Paul reveals the greatest difference—his conviction that God through his life and speech was calling people into the divine kingdom and glory. A complete portrayal of Paul as pastor will do justice to the theological dimension of Paul's understanding of his own task and of the nature of the little communities he founded, shaped, and nurtured.

# Index of Passages

# Index of Subjects